# Earth Watch

**Graeme Todd | Roger Palmer | Makimi Kano**

**NATIONAL
GEOGRAPHIC**
LEARNING

Australia · Brazil · Mexico · Singapore · United Kingdom · United States

**Earth Watch**

**Graeme Todd / Roger Palmer / Makimi Kano**

© 2020 Cengage Learning K.K.

**Video Credits:**
Unit 1: © AFP/STÉPHANE KOGUC, KATHERINE LEVY SPENCER; Unit 2: © AFP/STÉPHANE KOGUC, KATHERINE LEVY SPENCER; Unit 3: © AFP/STÉPHANE KOGUC, KATHERINE LEVY SPENCER; Unit 4: © AFP/DAVID LORY, EMMANUELLE BAILLON; Unit 5: © AFP/DAVID LORY, KATHERINE LEVY SPENCER; Unit 6: © AFP/MARIAN HENBEST, DAVID LORY; Unit 7: © AFP/FRED GARET; Unit 8: © AFP/STÉPHANE KOGUC, KATHERINE LEVY SPENCER; Unit 9: © AFP/STÉPHANE KOGUC, KATHERINE LEVY SPENCER; Unit 10: © AFP/FRED. GARET, KATHERINE LEVY SPENCER; Unit 11: © AFP/JONATHAN RENAUD DE LA FAVERIE, JONATHAN STOREY; Unit 12: © AFP/SABRINA BLANCHARD, KATHERINE SPENCER; Unit 13: © AFP/JONATHAN RENAUD DE LA FAVERIE, JONATHAN STOREY; Unit 14: © AFP/DAVID LORY, JONATHAN STOREY; Unit 15: © AFP/FRED GARET, KATHERINE LEVY SPENCER

Photo credits appear on page 99, which constitutes a continuation of the copyright page.

For permission to use material from this textbook or product, e-mail to **elt@cengagejapan.com**

ISBN: 978-4-86312-370-0

**National Geographic Learning | Cengage Learning K.K.**
No. 2 Funato Building 5th Floor
1-11-11 Kudankita, Chiyoda-ku
Tokyo 102-0073
Japan

Tel:  03-3511-4392
Fax:  03-3511-4391

# はしがき

　"Earth Watch" へようこそ。本書は英語の様々なスキルを駆使して、グローバル・イシューに関するテーマを理解し議論することを目的とする総合的なテキストです。私たちを取り巻く情勢は常に変化しています。気象変動や環境破壊、ゴミ問題や絶滅の危機に瀕する動物たちなど、近々に解決しなければならない問題は山積みです。一方で、技術革新や宇宙開発、代替エネルギーの登場や有機農法への関心の高まりなど、明るい将来を期待させる動きも活発になっています。このテキストは、今まさに注目されているこれらのテーマを素晴らしい映像と共に提示することで、みなさんが刺激を受けながら学習できるように作られています。見て、聞いて、読んで、コミュニケーションを取ることにより、アクティブな学習を体験することができます。

　"Earth Watch" では、世界中で現在広く議論されている自然環境や人類の未来に影響を与える 15 の現実社会の課題を取り上げて、現状を知り、これからどのようにしていくべきなのかじっくりと考えていきます。各ユニットはテーマに関する重要な語彙を押さえた上で、AFP 制作の動画を視聴し、私たちが直面している課題や現象について、現在どのような取り組みがなされているか学びます。動画を視聴したり、音声を聞いたりして内容を理解した後は、その動画の内容を簡潔にまとめた文章を読み、エクササイズに取り組むことで、さらに理解を深めます。情報を正確に伝えるためだけではなく、円滑なコミュニケーションのためのポイントを各ユニットで解説し、それを使ってテーマについての会話を練習します。クラスメイトなどからの意見の聞き取りを行い、賛成・反対の様々な立場の意見を検討した上で、自分の立場を確立させていきます。各ユニットの最後は個人的な意見や経験を共有しながら、自分の意見を論理的に組み立て発表し、グループでディスカッションを行います。

　これら一連の積極的な学びを英語で行うことによって、今まさに世界で注目され、取り組みが始まっている様々な課題や現象について英語で理解できるようになるだけでなく、それについて自分の立場・意見を英語で表明できるようになります。本書が、みなさんが真の国際人へと成長する一助となれば幸いです。

著者一同

# Table of Contents

# 本書の構成と使い方

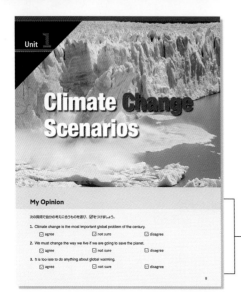

各ユニットは 6 ページ構成です。以下に、それぞれのアクティビティの内容と目的を説明します。

## My Opinion

ユニットで取り上げるトピックについて、**agree**、**not sure**、**disagree** の選択肢を選ぶ問題です。トピックに対する問題意識を高めます。

## Vocabulary Refresh

動画の中で使われている語句で、重要なものを取り上げています。英文に空欄を設け、右の語句リストから空欄に適切なものを入れ、音声 を聞いて、解答を確認します。ビデオを視聴する前に、重要な語句の意味と使い方をマスターします。

## First Watching

AFP 制作のビデオを視聴します。

動画の 80% ほどのスピードで音声を聞きます。

**A** 動画を視聴して、内容に近いほうの写真を選ぶ問題です。動画の内容の大まかな理解を確認します。

**B** 動画の内容に関して、重要なポイントを理解するための T/F 問題です。

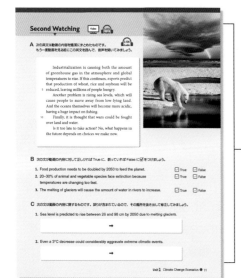

## Second Watching

First Watching と同じビデオをもう一度視聴して理解を深めます。

動画の 80% ほどのスピードで音声をもう一度聞き、理解を深めます。

**A** 動画の 2 度目の視聴をする前に、動画の内容を簡潔にまとめた英文を読み、音声 を聞き、動画のより深い理解をめざします。

**B** 動画の内容に関して、重要なポイントを理解するための T/F 問題です。

**C** 動画の内容に関する英文を読み、誤っている箇所を指摘する問題です。ビデオの内容の正確な理解をめざします。

## Communication Focus

英語でコミュニケーションをする際に、日本人学習者が意識して学習したほうがよい重要なポイントについて、例文を交えて解説しています。そこで取り上げた表現は **Model Conversation** に含まれています。実際の会話でどのように使われているかがわかります。

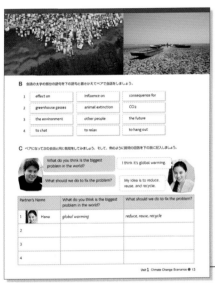

## Model Conversation

**A** 動画で取り上げたトピックについての会話を音声 🎧1-01 Audio で聞いて読みます。

**B** トピックについて話す際の重要な表現を別の語句に置きかえて、ペアで会話練習をします。

**C** サンプルの会話をペアになって行い、質問に対する相手の回答を書きます。トピックに関して、自分の意見を述べ、相手の意見を聞き、ポイントを書き取る練習をします。

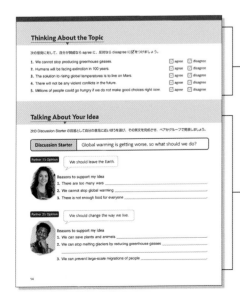

## Thinking About the Topic

トピックに関する意見を読んで、**agree** か **disagree** かを選び、自分の意見を明確にします。

## Talking About Your Idea

トピックに関する **Discussion Starter** の問題提起に対して、続く2つの意見のうち自分の意見に近いほうを選び、その意見を補足する英文を完成させ、グループで発表するアクティビティです。自分の意見を組み立てて、発表する練習をします。

## 動画ファイルの利用方法

 のアイコンがある箇所の動画ファイルにアクセスできます。

https://ngljapan.com/ew-audiovideo/video/

❶ 上記の URL にアクセス、または QR コードをスマートフォンなどのリーダーでスキャン

❷ 表示されるファイル名をクリックして動画ファイルを再生

## 音声ファイルの利用方法

 のアイコンがある箇所の音声ファイルにアクセスできます。

https://ngljapan.com/ew-audiovideo

❶ 上記の URL にアクセス、または QR コードをスマートフォンなどのリーダーでスキャン

❷ 表示されるファイル名をクリックして音声ファイルをダウンロードまたは再生

# Unit 1

# Climate Change Scenarios

## My Opinion

次の質問で自分の考えに合うものを選び、☑をつけましょう。

**1.** Climate change is the most important global problem of the century.

☑ agree        ☑ not sure        ☑ disagree

**2.** We must change the way we live if we are going to save the planet.

☑ agree        ☑ not sure        ☑ disagree

**3.** It is too late to do anything about global warming.

☑ agree        ☑ not sure        ☑ disagree

# Vocabulary Refresh

次の文の空欄に適切な語句を右の囲みから選んで入れましょう。完成したら、音声を聞いて確認しましょう。  1-02 Audio

1. Global warming is caused by _____ such as $CO_2$ in _____.

2. Many plants and animals are _____ because of global warming.

3. Experts tell us that _____ have been going up since _____.

4. Extreme _____ include heat waves, droughts, tornadoes, and hurricanes.

5. The _____ of global warming could also cause _____ over territory or water.

6. Global warming will have a _____ on _____ as the production of crops is reduced.

**Vocabulary Box Items**

climatic events
cumulative effects
devastating impact
facing extinction
food security
global temperatures
greenhouse gasses
the atmosphere
the onset of industrialization
violent conflicts

# First Watching

 Video  1-03 Audio

**A** 次の写真のうち、動画の中で述べられている内容に近いほうを選び、☑をつけましょう。

☑

☑

**B** 次の文が動画の内容に対して正しければ True、誤まっていれば False に ☑をつけましょう。

1. It is possible that global temperatures could rise by 5°C by 2100.　　☑True　☑False

2. By 2050 the population will have grown by about 90 million people.　　☑True　☑False

3. By making the right choices now we can avoid global warming.　　☑True　☑False

# Second Watching

**A** 次の英文は動画の内容を簡潔にまとめたものです。
もう一度動画を見る前にこの英文を読んで、音声を聞いてみましょう。

Industrialization is causing both the amount of greenhouse gas in the atmosphere and global temperatures to rise. If this continues, experts predict that production of wheat, rice and soybean will be
5  reduced, leaving millions of people hungry.
Another problem is rising sea levels, which will cause people to move away from low-lying land. And the oceans themselves will become more acidic, having a huge impact on fishing.
10  Finally, it is thought that wars could be fought over land and water.
Is it too late to take action? No, what happens in the future depends on choices we make now.

**B** 次の文が動画の内容に対して正しければ True に、誤っていれば False に ☑ をつけましょう。

1. Food production needs to be doubled by 2050 to feed the planet.　　☑ True　☑ False

2. 20–30% of animal and vegetable species face extinction because
   temperatures are changing too fast.　　☑ True　☑ False

3. The melting of glaciers will cause the amount of water in rivers to increase.　　☑ True　☑ False

**C** 次の文は動画の内容に関するものです。誤りが含まれているので、その箇所を抜き出して修正してみましょう。

1. Sea level is predicted to rise between 26 and 98 cm by 2050 due to melting glaciers.

　　　　　　　　　➡

2. Even a 3°C decrease could considerably aggravate extreme climatic events.

　　　　　　　　　➡

### agreeing/disagreeing 意見の一致・不一致

英語はストレートに何でも言っていい言語と思われがちですが、必ずしもそうではありません。特に人の意見に反対するときには、相手を傷つけないようにクッションをおいてから自分の意見を述べます。Yes, that's true, but .... 「それは事実なんだけど…」や You have a point there, but ... 「君の言うことには一理あるんだけど…」のようにいったん相手の意見を肯定的に受け止めてから、自分の意見を切り出すといいでしょう。

■ A: I don't think it's right to keep your dog in such a small cage.
　　　「犬をそんな小さなケージに閉じ込めておくなんてよくないと思う。」
　　B: I see your point. But I can't let him walk in my room freely while I'm away.
　　　「言っていることはわかるよ。でも、留守中家の中を自由に歩かせるわけにもいかないんだ。」

逆に、同意するときには、はっきりと同じ意見であることを表明します。Yeah, で始めるだけで、同意する気持ちが伝わりますし、I agree with you. 「私も同じ意見です。」や I guess you are right. 「あなたが言っていることは正しいと思います。」と率直に伝えるのもいいでしょう。Exactly! 「まさに！」や That's what I was thinking! 「同じことを考えていた！」、That sounds great! 「素晴らしい考えだよ！」のように少し大げさなくらいの表現を使うのも好印象です。

## Model Conversation

A　音声を聞きながら、次の会話を読んでみましょう。 🎧 1-05 Audio

Bill: My friend told me about diving in the Caribbean. It sounded really exciting.

Kate: Yes, but flying there will have a bad ¹**impact on** the atmosphere.

Bill: I guess you're right. Do you mean a big problem like
²**global warming**?

Kate: Exactly! It's a serious issue right now.

Bill: Yeah, I suppose we should think more about ³**the Earth**.

Kate: Is there anywhere else you would like to go?

Bill: We could go camping.

Kate: That sounds nice.
We will have lots of time
⁴**to talk** when we get there.

**B** **A** の会話の太字部分の語句を下の語句と置きかえてペアで会話をしましょう。

| | | | |
|---|---|---|---|
| 1 | effect on | influence on | consequence for |
| 2 | greenhouse gasses | animal extinction | CO2 |
| 3 | the environment | other people | the future |
| 4 | to chat | to relax | to hang out |

**C** ペアになって次の会話と同じ質問をしてみましょう。そして、例のように質問の回答を下の表に記入しましょう。

What do you think is the biggest problem in the world?

I think it's global warming.

What should we do to fix the problem?

My idea is to reduce, reuse, and recycle.

| Partner's Name | What do you think is the biggest problem in the world? | What should we do to fix the problem? |
|---|---|---|
| 1   Hana | *global warming* | *reduce, reuse, recycle* |
| 2 | | |
| 3 | | |
| 4 | | |

# Thinking About the Topic

次の意見に対して、自分が賛成なら agree に、反対なら disagree に☑をつけましょう。

1. We cannot stop producing greenhouse gasses. ☑ agree ☑ disagree
2. Humans will be facing extinction in 100 years. ☑ agree ☑ disagree
3. The solution to rising global temperatures is to live on Mars. ☑ agree ☑ disagree
4. There will not be any violent conflicts in the future. ☑ agree ☑ disagree
5. Millions of people could go hungry if we do not make good choices right now. ☑ agree ☑ disagree

# Talking About Your Idea

次の Discussion Starter の回答として自分の意見に近いほうを選び、その英文を完成させ、ペアかグループで発表しましょう。

| **Discussion Starter** | Global warming is getting worse, so what should we do? |
|---|---|

**Partner 1's Opinion**

We should leave the Earth.

### Reasons to support my idea

1. There are too many wars _____.
2. We cannot stop global warming _____.
3. There is not enough food for everyone _____.

**Partner 2's Opinion**

We should change the way we live.

### Reasons to support my idea

1. We can save plants and animals _____.
2. We can stop melting glaciers by reducing greenhouse gasses _____
_____.
3. We can prevent large-scale migrations of people _____.

# Unit 2

# Artificial Intelligence

## My Opinion

次の質問で自分の考えに合うものを選び、☑をつけましょう。

**1.** Robots will one day do all the work of nurses in hospitals.

☑ agree          ☑ not sure          ☑ disagree

**2.** Artificial intelligence will soon cause a lot of unemployment.

☑ agree          ☑ not sure          ☑ disagree

**3.** Artificial intelligence will never be smarter than the human brain in every way.

☑ agree          ☑ not sure          ☑ disagree

# Vocabulary Refresh

次の文の空欄に適切な語句を右の囲みから選んで入れましょう。完成したら、音声を聞いて確認しましょう。

1. Technological advances have seen AI take _____ _____ and become a part of our daily lives.

2. _____ could increase road safety by _____ of human error.

3. In the future robots will do _____ humans should not or will not do.

4. In medicine, _____ can already _____ _____ such as cancer.

5. _____ could be threatened as robots _____ of nearly everything humans do.

6. A lot needs to be done before robots have the same level of _____ _____ as humans.

**Vocabulary Box Items**

autonomous vehicles

become capable

diagnose illnesses

eliminating the risk

great strides forward

hazardous jobs

millions of jobs

social intelligence

software

---

# First Watching

Video | 1-07 Audio

**A** 次の写真のうち、動画の中で述べられている内容に近いほうを選び、☑をつけましょう。

**B** 次の文が動画の内容に対して正しければ True、誤まっていれば False に ☑をつけましょう。

1. Smartphones will soon be replaced by robot assistants. ☑ True ☑ False

2. Super-intelligent computers might be a threat to humanity. ☑ True ☑ False

3. Some experts think AI will become smarter than humans in the next few years. ☑ True ☑ False

16

# Second Watching

**A** 次の英文は動画の内容を簡潔にまとめたものです。
もう一度動画を見る前にこの英文を読んで、音声を聞いてみましょう。

1-08 Audio

Artificial intelligence is about creating computers and machines that learn and make decisions as well as humans. It offers the possibility of a wonderful future in which robots take care of the sick, drive
5 cars, and do all the dangerous jobs.

Machines are already smart enough to win at games like chess and software can diagnose some illnesses as well as a real doctor. But what will we do when robots become smart enough to replace
10 humans in the workforce?

Some experts also think that super-intelligent computers and robots could be dangerous if they become smarter than people. Will they want to take control?

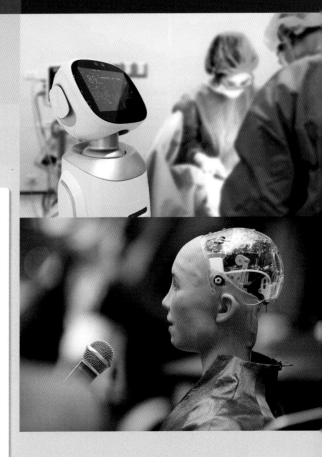

**B** 次の文が動画の内容に対して正しければ True に、誤っていれば False に ☑ をつけましょう。

1. Artificial intelligence is already becoming part of daily life.  ☑ True  ☑ False

2. Some doctors have lost their jobs because of artificial intelligence.  ☑ True  ☑ False

3. Robot surgeons will be working in our hospitals quite soon.  ☑ True  ☑ False

**C** 次の文は動画の内容に関するものです。誤りが含まれているので、その箇所を抜き出して修正してみましょう。

1. Artificial intelligence—or AI—is the science of programming robots to reproduce human processes.

➡

2. AI offers the promise of a very modern world in which robots take care of our sick.

➡

## discussing probabilities 可能性について話す

　この先に起きる出来事の様々な可能性を語る方法は大きく分けて2つあります。1つは推量の助動詞を用いることです。可能性が非常に低いと思うなら could、might、may を、可能性が高いと思うなら should、確実だと思うなら must、will を使います。仮定の話のときには、will ではなく would を使います。例えば、次の通りです。

天気予報の降水確率が 30% のとき

　■ It might rain later today. 「今日は後で雨が降るかもね。」

天気予報の降水確率が 90% のとき

　■ It should rain later today. 「今日は後で雨が降るはずだよ。」

　もう1つは副詞です。definitely、surely、certainly は自信を持った予測に、probably ならほぼ確実なときに、likely はもう少し確率が低い時に使います。possibly、perhaps、maybe は低い可能性を表します。これらの副詞は上記の推量の助動詞としばしば一緒に用いられます。could、might と possibly、should と probably、will、would、must と certainly などです。

　■ They may possibly come soon. 「ひょっとしたら彼らはもうすぐやって来るかもしれない。」

　■ She will probably come. 「彼女は十中八九来るだろう。」

# Model Conversation

**A**　音声を聞きながら、次の会話を読んでみましょう。  1-09 Audio

Yumi: I am concerned about my future.

Ken: You'll be fine!

Yumi: I mean, with all this technology do you think I can find a job?

Ken: Sure, don't worry. Actually, I think AI will make our lives better.

Yumi: But won't ¹**AI** replace workers?

Ken: I don't know. Some ²**jobs** might be lost. But it could have some advantages too.

Yumi: Possibly. And I suppose I'd have more time for ³**meeting friends**.

Ken: Yeah, and you'd ⁴**probably** live a happier life.

**B** Aの会話の太字部分の語句を下の語句と置きかえてペアで会話をしましょう。

| | | | |
|---|---|---|---|
| 1 | computers | technology | robots |
| 2 | work | occupations | professions |
| 3 | playing tennis | my hobbies | chilling out |
| 4 | certainly | definitely | surely |

**C** ペアになって次の会話と同じ質問をしてみましょう。そして、例のように質問の回答を下の表に記入しましょう。

Is artificial intelligence a good thing?

Yes, because it can help the sick.

Will humans need to work in the future?

Probably not!

| Partner's Name | Is artificial intelligence a good thing? | Will humans need to work in the future? |
|---|---|---|
| 1　Guy | *Yes – helps the sick* | *Probably not!* |
| 2 | | |
| 3 | | |
| 4 | | |

# Thinking About the Topic

次の意見に対して、自分が賛成なら agree に、反対なら disagree に ☑ をつけましょう。

1. Robots will take care of the sick.      ☑ agree ☑ disagree
2. Software is going to cure illnesses.      ☑ agree ☑ disagree
3. AI will take away jobs from people.      ☑ agree ☑ disagree
4. Robots may become smarter than humans.      ☑ agree ☑ disagree
5. We need to stop computers from taking control of the world.      ☑ agree ☑ disagree

# Talking About Your Idea

次の Discussion Starter の回答として自分の意見に近いほうを選び、その英文を完成させ、ペアかグループで発表しましょう。

| **Discussion Starter** | Artificial intelligence is making robots smarter than humans. |
|---|---|

**Partner 1's Opinion**

> Robots will help humans more and more.

**Reasons to support my idea**

1. Robots can take care of old people _____.
2. They will give us more free time _____.
3. They can do all the dirty and dangerous work _____.

**Partner 2's Opinion**

> Robots could take over the world.

**Reasons to support my idea**

1. Robots will be even more intelligent _____.
2. They could be used as weapons _____.
3. They will control humans _____.

# Endangered Species

## My Opinion

次の質問で自分の考えに合うものを選び、☑をつけましょう。

**1.** The buying and selling of all endangered species should be made illegal.

☑ agree          ☑ not sure          ☑ disagree

**2.** I would not eat the meat of an endangered animal or sea creature.

☑ agree          ☑ not sure          ☑ disagree

**3.** Wild animals are endangered because the human population of our planet has become too large.

☑ agree          ☑ not sure          ☑ disagree

# Vocabulary Refresh

次の文の空欄に適切な語句を右の囲みから選んで入れましょう。完成したら、音声を聞いて確認しましょう。  1-10 Audio

1. A quarter of all _____ are currently _____ of disappearing entirely from our planet.

2. Antarctic blue whales, the largest creatures on the planet, are _____.

3. Freshwater species such as crocodiles, hippos, and river dolphins are _____ as threatened.

4. The pangolin is _____ because in Asia it is used in _____.

5. Many primates are under threat of extinction due to _____ _____.

6. Rhinoceros _____ are threatened, primarily by _____.

**Vocabulary Box Items**

at risk

classified

critically endangered

habitat destruction

in the wild

mammals

poaching

traditional medicine

trafficked

# First Watching   Video   1-11 Audio

**A** 次の写真のうち、動画の中で述べられている内容に近いほうを選び、☑をつけましょう。

a

b

☑                                                                ☑

**B** 次の文が動画の内容に対して正しければ True、誤まっていれば False に ☑をつけましょう。

1. More than 40% of amphibians are at risk of disappearing from our planet.   ☑ True   ☑ False

2. Coral reefs—home to over a quarter of all amphibians—could disappear by 2060.   ☑ True   ☑ False

3. Four out of six of the Earth's great apes are endangered or critically endangered.   ☑ True   ☑ False

# Second Watching

Video | 1-11 Audio

**A** 次の英文は動画の内容を簡潔にまとめたものです。
もう一度動画を見る前にこの英文を読んで、音声を聞いてみましょう。

1-12 Audio

Scientists think Earth could be experiencing its first "mass extinction event" since the dinosaurs died out, with many species endangered due to human activity and climate change.

5　In the oceans, blue whales are just a step away from dying out. But the vaquita, a porpoise, is probably closest to extinction. It gets caught in fishing nets and drowns.

Back on land, more than half of all primates are under threat of extinction and rhinoceros are seriously
10　endangered.

Additionally, the number of elephants has fallen quickly and the giant panda remains vulnerable.

Finally, the future of six out of eight bear species is also a cause for concern.

**B** 次の文が動画の内容に対して正しければ True に、誤っていれば False に ☑ をつけましょう。

1. The last "mass extinction event" on Earth occurred about 65 million years ago. ☑ True ☑ False

2. Animals and marine creatures almost always become extinct because of climate change. ☑ True ☑ False

3. There are no northern white rhinos left on Earth. ☑ True ☑ False

**C** 次の文は動画の内容に関するものです。誤りが含まれているので、その箇所を抜き出して修正してみましょう。

1. Life in the oceans has been less endangered by human activity and climate change.

➡

2. The vaquita, the world's smallest porpoise, is probably the species most safe from extinction.

➡

## Communication Focus

### giving opinions　意見を述べる

　時事的なテーマから日常的な話題まで、What do you think about ...?「…についてどう思う？」と自身の意見を求められることはよくあります。その際は、I don't know.「わからない。」などと曖昧な返事をするのではなく、何かしら自分の意見を表明するようにしましょう。I think、I suppose、I believe、I guess ...「…だと思う。」などを言い始めに使います。In my opinion, ...「私の意見では、…」と始めてもいいでしょう。もし十分な知識があるわけではないテーマについて聞かれたときは、I'm not sure, but ...「はっきりとは分からないけど…」や I'm not familiar with the issue, but ...「この問題についてよく知らないんだけれども…」など、前置きをしてから述べるといいでしょう。

　■ I don't know much about painting, but I think this is beautiful.
　　「絵のことはよく分からないけど、これは美しいと思う。」

　賛成意見を表すときには、I agree with/support/approve of ...「…に賛成です。」を使ってはっきりと、反対意見を表すときは、相手と真正面から対立するのは避け、I <u>kind of</u> disagree with ...「…と<u>ちょっと</u>違う意見です。」や I'm <u>not totally</u> in agreement with ...「…と<u>全く</u>同じ意見<u>というわけではありません。</u>」のように垣根表現（hedge）を使うほうが議論がスムーズに進むでしょう。

## Model Conversation

A　音声を聞きながら、次の会話を読んでみましょう。  13 Audio

　Del: I am thinking of entering the college debating contest.

　Ruby: Cool! I think you'd do really well.

　Del: Really? The topic seems ¹**kind of tough** though.

　Ruby: Is it? What are you debating?

　Del: It's about the problem of animal poaching.

　Ruby: I see. What do you think about ²**poaching**?

　Del: Well, I ³**support** a ban … but in the debate I would have to argue against it.

　Ruby: ⁴**Oh**! I can't really help you with that.

**B** Aの会話の太字部分の語句を下の語句と置きかえてペアで会話をしましょう。

| 1 | difficult | hard | tricky |
| 2 | hunting | trafficking | killing animals |
| 3 | agree with | am in favor of | approve of |
| 4 | Gosh | Wow | Holy cow |

**C** ペアになって次の会話と同じ質問をしてみましょう。そして、例のように質問の回答を下の表に記入しましょう。

What's your favorite animal?

What do think about hunting?

That's easy. I love dogs.

I think it's okay to hunt deer, but not dogs!

| Partner's Name | What's your favorite animal? | What do think about hunting? |
|---|---|---|
| 1   Boris | *dogs* | *deer, yes; dogs, no* |
| 2 | | |
| 3 | | |
| 4 | | |

# Thinking About the Topic

次の意見に対して、自分が賛成なら agree に、反対なら disagree に☑をつけましょう。

1. Many animals are endangered.    ☑ agree   ☑ disagree

2. Humans should protect animals.    ☑ agree   ☑ disagree

3. We need animal products for medicines and cosmetics.    ☑ agree   ☑ disagree

4. I have the right to eat any food I like.    ☑ agree   ☑ disagree

5. We should try harder to stop poaching.    ☑ agree   ☑ disagree

# Talking About Your Idea

次の Discussion Starter の回答として自分の意見に近いほうを選び、その英文を完成させ、ペアかグループで発表しましょう。

| **Discussion Starter** | The human population of our planet is too large. |
|---|---|

**Partner 1's Opinion**

There are certainly too many people in the world.

### Reasons to support my idea

1. With more people, we eat too much _____.

2. All countries are fishing in the sea _____.

3. Wild animals have nowhere to live _____.

**Partner 2's Opinion**

I'm not sure there are too many people.

### Reasons to support my idea

1. Some villages have no one living in them _____.

2. There are mainly old people in some towns _____.

3. There are not enough workers _____.

# Unit 4

# Journey into Space

## My Opinion

次の質問で自分の考えに合うものを選び、☑をつけましょう。

1. I would like to travel into space.

   ☑ agree            ☑ not sure            ☑ disagree

2. Living in space could cause a lot of health problems.

   ☑ agree            ☑ not sure            ☑ disagree

3. It will never be possible for humans to survive in space for long periods.

   ☑ agree            ☑ not sure            ☑ disagree

# Vocabulary Refresh

次の文の空欄に適切な語句を右の囲みから選んで入れましょう。完成したら、音声を聞いて確認しましょう。

1. For humans, space is a _____ place.

2. The biggest _____ are cosmic radiation and
   _____.

3. Muscles lose up to 20% of their _____ in a few days.

4. The _____ can lengthen up to 5 cm.

5. Exposure to _____ in space increases the risk of
   _____.

6. The loneliness of _____ can also affect morale and
   _____.

**Vocabulary Box Items**

backbone
cancer
cause stress
challenges
hostile
mass
microgravity
radiation
space flight

# First Watching

**A** 次の写真のうち、動画の中で述べられている内容に近いほうを選び、☑をつけましょう。

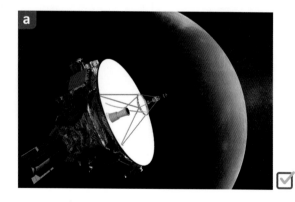

**B** 次の文が動画の内容に対して正しければ True、誤まっていれば False に ☑をつけましょう。

1. In space, bone density drops by 1 to 1.5% in a single month. ☑ True ☑ False

2. In just six months the heart can age between 10 and 20 years. ☑ True ☑ False

3. On a mission to Mars, astronauts could be in space for up to nine months. ☑ True ☑ False

# Second Watching

Video

**A** 次の英文は動画の内容を簡潔にまとめたものです。
もう一度動画を見る前にこの英文を読んで、音声を聞いてみましょう。

> For humans, space is an unfriendly place and the biggest challenges are cosmic radiation and microgravity.
> Microgravity affects body functions, causing
> 5 problems with bone density, the muscles, the heart and arteries.
> Earth's atmosphere protects humans from cosmic radiation, but in space it poses a real threat. It increases the risk of cancer and alters the blood
> 10 count and the immune system.
> Another problem is the loneliness of space flight. This can affect morale and cause stress.
> This is all a lot to cope with, especially on long missions when astronauts could be in space for
> 15 months at a time.

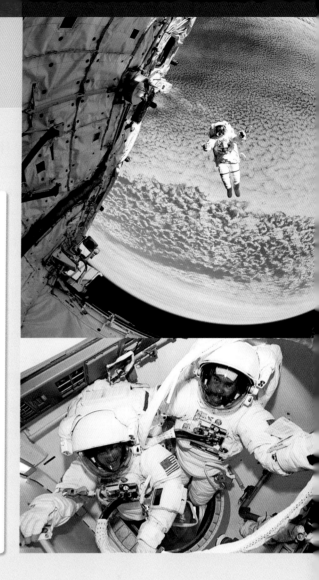

**B** 次の文が動画の内容に対して正しければ True に、誤っていれば False に ☑ をつけましょう。

1. In space the human heart does not need to work so hard. ☑ True ☑ False

2. Being in space for short periods improves human vision. ☑ True ☑ False

3. For health reasons, humans will never be able to travel to Mars. ☑ True ☑ False

**C** 次の文は動画の内容に関するものです。誤りが含まれているので、その箇所を抜き出して修正してみましょう。

1. In space, body fluids travel to the head, putting pressure on the arteries.

   ➡

2. Exposure to radiation on the International Space Station is a little greater than on Earth.

   ➡

## Communication Focus

### describing people, places, things, experiences　人・場所・もの・経験を描写する

面接などで Tell me about yourself.「あなたのことを教えてください。」と言われ、自分がどんな人物なのか描写しなければならない場面はよくあります。「～県生まれ、～高校出身です。」と、自分の過去のデータを並べてもつまらないですから、I am ....、I like ....、I enjoy ....、I'm good at ....、I'm interested in .... など、今の自分がどんな人物なのかを中心に語りましょう。

■ I am an outgoing person. I like to travel abroad. I enjoy talking with people. I'm good at making friends.
「私は外向的な性格です。海外旅行が好きです。人と話すのが楽しいです。友達を作るのが得意です。」

その上で、その人物像をサポートするような場所、もの、経験の描写を付け加えると効果的です。

■ Last summer, I traveled to the Philippines to take part in some volunteer activities, and met a lot of local people and people from all over the world there. We talked for a long time every day and became good friends.「去年の夏、ボランティア活動に参加するためフィリピンに行きました。そこでたくさんの地元の人や世界中から来た人に会いました。毎日長い時間話して、いい友達になりました。」

人にはもちろん弱点や短所もありますが、できるだけポジティブな面を押し出すのがいいでしょう。I'm shy. I'm not good at talking in front of people.「私は恥ずかしがり屋で、人前で話すのは得意ではありません。」のような自信のなさをわざわざ露呈するような描写は特に英語では避けましょう。

# Model Conversation

A　音声を聞きながら、次の会話を読んでみましょう。  1-17 Audio

Anne-Marie: Hey Bjorn, I have to fill out a survey about staying healthy. It asks me to describe my lifestyle.

Bjorn: Well, what have you written so far?

Anne-Marie: I do yoga to avoid stress. I enjoy ¹**challenges**. I am afraid of dogs.

Bjorn: That sounds okay. What's next?

Anne-Marie: It asks me what I'd most like to do.

Bjorn: I know! I want a real challenge, like ²**going into space**.

Anne-Marie: But for me, I'm not sure that's ³**realistic**.

Bjorn: Oh sorry, it was just ⁴**an idea**.

**B** Aの会話の太字部分の語句を下の語句と置きかえてペアで会話をしましょう。

| | | | |
|---|---|---|---|
| 1 | excitement | variety | new situations |
| 2 | traveling to the Sun | living on the Moon | flying a spaceship |
| 3 | practical | possible | going to happen |
| 4 | a thought | my own dream | something I imagined |

**C** ペアになって次の会話と同じ質問をしてみましょう。そして、例のように質問の回答を下の表に記入しましょう。

What's the worst thing about stress?

What's a good cure for stress?

My shoulders ache.

I find playing sports helps.

| Partner's Name | What's the worst thing about stress? | What's a good cure for stress? |
|---|---|---|
| 1   Lee | *shoulder ache* | *playing sports* |
| 2 | | |
| 3 | | |
| 4 | | |

# Thinking About the Topic

次の意見に対して、自分が賛成なら agree に、反対なら disagree に☑をつけましょう。

1. Humans should live on Earth, not in space. ☑ agree ☑ disagree
2. I would like to go to a place with no gravity. ☑ agree ☑ disagree
3. If I go into space, I will live much longer. ☑ agree ☑ disagree
4. Life will be better in the future. ☑ agree ☑ disagree
5. Space travel is bad for our health. ☑ agree ☑ disagree

# Talking About Your Idea

次の Discussion Starter の回答として自分の意見に近いほうを選び、その英文を完成させ、ペアかグループで発表しましょう。

| **Discussion Starter** | Space travel will be as easy as riding a bus. |
|---|---|

**Partner 1's Opinion**

Technology will solve the problems.

**Reasons to support my idea**

1. Space travel will be more comfortable _____.
2. We will fly at the speed of light _____.
3. Spaceships will fly themselves _____.

**Partner 2's Opinion**

There are still some risks.

**Reasons to support my idea**

1. No one has lived in space for long _____.
2. There are health problems _____.
3. Stress may make us unhappy _____.

# Australia's Great Barrier Reef

## My Opinion

次の質問で自分の考えに合うものを選び、☑をつけましょう。

**1.** I would be very interested in taking a trip to Australia's Great Barrier Reef.

☑ agree          ☑ not sure          ☑ disagree

**2.** I am very concerned about the health of the world's oceans and coral reefs.

☑ agree          ☑ not sure          ☑ disagree

**3.** Popular sites like the Great Barrier Reef should restrict the number of tourist visitors.

☑ agree          ☑ not sure          ☑ disagree

# Vocabulary Refresh

次の文の空欄に適切な語句を右の囲みから選んで入れましょう。完成したら、音声を聞いて確認しましょう。 🎧 1-18 Audio

1. Australia's Great Barrier Reef is the world's biggest coral _____.

2. Global warming is _____ on the Great Barrier Reef, threatening its very _____.

3. Bleaching occurs when abnormal _____ _____ cause corals to expel photosynthetic algae.

4. Bleaching itself does not kill the reefs, but they become more _____ _____.

5. Reefs need some 15 years to _____ from bleaching of this _____.

6. The Great Barrier Reef supports a multi-billion dollar _____ _____ and _____ of jobs.

**Vocabulary Box Items**

- completely recover
- ecosystem
- environmental conditions
- magnitude
- survival
- tens of thousands
- tourist industry
- vulnerable to disease
- wreaking havoc

# First Watching  [Video] 🎧 1-19 Audio

**A** 次の写真のうち、動画の中で述べられている内容に近いほうを選び、☑をつけましょう。

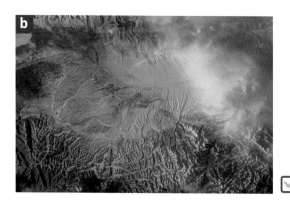

**B** 次の文が動画の内容に対して正しければ True、誤っていれば False に ☑をつけましょう。

1. Australia's Great Barrier Reef, the world's biggest coral ecosystem, is no longer visible from space.　☑ True　☑ False

2. Australia's Great Barrier Reef is a World Heritage-listed site.　☑ True　☑ False

3. Large parts of the Great Barrier Reef could be lost within 10 years.　☑ True　☑ False

# Second Watching

**A** 次の英文は動画の内容を簡潔にまとめたものです。
もう一度動画を見る前にこの英文を読んで、音声を聞いてみましょう。

1-20 Audio

Australia's Great Barrier Reef is huge. It spans nearly 350,000 square kilometers and can be seen from space.

But global warming threatens its very survival. The problem is bleaching. This occurs when abnormal
5 environmental conditions, especially warmer sea temperatures, cause coral to lose its color.

Experts say that if greenhouse gasses keep rising, bleaching will become a regular event and large parts of the Great Barrier Reef could be lost within just a couple
10 of decades.

Urgent government action is needed to improve water quality or the reef could soon be beyond saving.

**B** 次の文が動画の内容に対して正しければ True に、誤っていれば False に ☑ をつけましょう。

1. Australia's Great Barrier Reef contains 600 types of coral and 1,500 species of fish.    ☑ True    ☑ False

2. The dugong (known as the "sea cow") and the large green turtle are threatened with extinction.    ☑ True    ☑ False

3. If greenhouse gasses keep rising, bleaching events will occur every two years by the mid-2030s.    ☑ True    ☑ False

**C** 次の文は動画の内容に関するものです。誤りが含まれているので、その箇所を抜き出して修正してみましょう。

1. In 2016, the reef experienced its first bleaching, with some 93% of corals affected.

➡

2. Aside from climate change, other threats to the reef include farming run-off and tourism.

➡

# Communication Focus

## giving advice　助言をする

　人にアドバイスをするときは、Why don't you ...? や Why not ...?「〜してみてはどうですか?」を使うのが一般的です。自分も一緒にすることについての助言なら Why don't we ...?、話し手が相手のためにすることについてなら Why don't I ...? になります。

- ■ If you want to know about Japan, why don't you go there?「日本のことを知りたいなら、行ってみたら?」
- ■ Why don't we take a taxi together to save some money?「節約のために一緒にタクシーに乗りましょうか?」
- ■ Why don't I lend you my bicycle while I'm away?「留守中、私の自転車を使ったら?」

　ただし、why を使った表現は、言い方によっては「なぜそうしないのか?」と理由を問いただしているとも捉えられかねないので、言い方を和らげたいときには、You might want to .... を使うといいでしょう。直訳すると「あなたは〜したいかもしれない。」と変な日本語ですが、「ひょっとして〜してみるといいかもよ。」のように押しつけない感じでアドバイスできるので便利です。

# Model Conversation

**A**　音声を聞きながら、次の会話を読んでみましょう。 🎧 1-21 Audio

Diana: I'm thinking of getting a job as a tour guide.

Jerry: Uh huh. You'd be good at that.

Diana: But I'm worried about the damage that tourism causes.

Jerry: I know what you mean. We all ¹**affect** the environment.

Diana: But I think I could do the job ²**responsibly**.

Jerry: Of course you could. Why don't you look for a tour company that agrees with your ³**principles**?

Diana: Good ⁴**idea**, I will. How about you?

Jerry: Me, a tour guide? No way! I can't even read a map!

**B** **A** の会話の太字部分の語句を下の語句と置きかえてペアで会話をしましょう。

| 1 | influence | have an effect on | change |
|---|-----------|-------------------|--------|
| 2 | really well | sensibly | nicely |
| 3 | views | beliefs | ideals |
| 4 | suggestion | advice | tip |

**C** ペアになって次の会話と同じ質問をしてみましょう。そして、例のように質問の回答を下の表に記入しましょう。

What do you think about group tours?

Do tourists damage the places they visit?

They seem like an easy way to travel.

I suppose so, if there are too many of them.

| Partner's Name | What do you think about group tours? | Do tourists damage the places they visit? |
|----------------|--------------------------------------|-------------------------------------------|
| 1   Jake | *easy way to travel* | *Yes–if too many* |
| 2 | | |
| 3 | | |
| 4 | | |

# Thinking About the Topic

次の意見に対して、自分が賛成なら agree に、反対なら disagree に☑をつけましょう。

1. Coral is beautiful to look at. ☑ agree ☑ disagree

2. Global warming damages coral. ☑ agree ☑ disagree

3. Tourism always has benefits. ☑ agree ☑ disagree

4. The Great Barrier Reef is more important than other reefs. ☑ agree ☑ disagree

5. The Great Barrier Reef is important for jobs. ☑ agree ☑ disagree

# Talking About Your Idea

次の Discussion Starter の回答として自分の意見に近いほうを選び、その英文を完成させ、ペアかグループで発表しましょう。

| **Discussion Starter** | The tourist industry helps local people. |
| --- | --- |

**Partner 1's Opinion**

Tourists support our local economy.

### Reasons to support my idea

1. Tourists buy souvenirs _____.
2. Tourists eat in local restaurants _____.
3. Local people find jobs in hotels _____.

**Partner 2's Opinion**

I sometimes think there are too many tourists.

### Reasons to support my idea

1. Tourist buses cause pollution _____.
2. Tourists throw trash on the streets _____.
3. Shops become too crowded _____.

# Unit 6

# Self-driving Cars

## My Opinion

次の質問で自分の考えに合うものを選び、☑をつけましょう。

**1.** Most of us will be using self-driving cars within the next 20 years.

☑ agree      ☑ not sure      ☑ disagree

**2.** I would not feel safe as a passenger in a self-driving car.

☑ agree      ☑ not sure      ☑ disagree

**3.** Many professional drivers will lose their jobs because of self-driving cars.

☑ agree      ☑ not sure      ☑ disagree

# Vocabulary Refresh

次の文の空欄に適切な語句を右の囲みから選んで入れましょう。完成したら、音声を聞いて確認しましょう。

1. _____ cars have eyes in all places.

2. The car's _____ is linked up to an

   _____.

3. The camera _____ the road ahead for _____ and calculates distances.

4. A variety of radars are used _____ close or distant objects.

5. The car is also fitted with sensors like rain _____.

6. _____ keep the car on the road in case of heavy gusts and _____.

### Vocabulary Box Items

- autonomous
- detectors
- gales
- obstacles
- onboard computer
- scans
- stereo camera
- to sense
- wind meters

# First Watching

**A** 次の写真のうち、動画の中で述べられている内容に近いほうを選び、☑をつけましょう。

**B** 次の文が動画の内容に対して正しければ True、誤っていれば False に ☑をつけましょう。

1. Self-driving cars have many cameras, radars and sensors.    ☑ True   ☑ False

2. The car's stereo camera is located on the roof.    ☑ True   ☑ False

3. Radars allow the car to sense objects up to 200 meters away.    ☑ True   ☑ False

# Second Watching

**A** 次の英文は動画の内容を簡潔にまとめたものです。
もう一度動画を見る前にこの英文を読んで、音声を聞いてみましょう。

1-24 Audio

A self-driving car is fitted with numerous cameras, radars and sensors.

At the heart of the system is a stereo camera, which is linked to an onboard computer. This camera
5  scans the road ahead for obstacles and calculates distances.

Other cameras on the vehicle scan the rest of the road. They read traffic light signals and road signs.

Small radars on the sides check around the
10  vehicle, for cyclists riding alongside for example, and the car is also fitted with rain detectors and wind meters. These keep the car on the road in case of strong winds.

**B** 次の文が動画の内容に対して正しければ True に、誤っていれば False に ☑ をつけましょう。

1. The car's 360-vision exceeds the relatively limited view of a driver using mirrors.   ☑ True   ☑ False

2. The car's onboard computer is placed where the driver usually sits.   ☑ True   ☑ False

3. Bicycles will also be fitted with small radars to increase safety.   ☑ True   ☑ False

**C** 次の文は動画の内容に関するものです。誤りが含まれているので、その箇所を抜き出して修正してみましょう。

1. The computer can recognize dangerous objects like a child running into the road.

          ➡

2. The car is fitted with sensors like rain detectors, which control windows and air-conditioning.

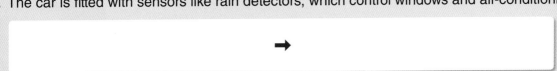

          ➡

# Communication Focus

## offering encouragement 励ます

　円滑なコミュニケーションの基本は、相手に心地よく感じてもらうことです。少し難しい状況のとき、You are good.「大丈夫。」You are doing well.「うまくやってるよ。」と現状を認めてもらうだけでも、もっと頑張ろうという気持ちになれます。You are such a good driver.「運転上手だね。」のように具体的な動作を褒めるとよりいいでしょう。英語ではわざわざへりくだることはありませんが、本当にそう思うなら、You're a much better driver than I am.「私よりずっと運転がうまいね。」と自分と比べて相手の優れている点を強調するのもいいでしょう。

　日本語の「頑張って。」は非常に便利な励ましの表現ですが、すべての場合に通用する１つの英語表現があるわけではありません。意味合いは異なりますが、Good luck.「うまく行きますように。」が場面的には一番当てはまる範囲が広いでしょう。You can do it.「君ならできる。」You'll be all right.「うまく行くよ。」と自信を持ってもらうために、積極的に励ますのも効果的です。

# Model Conversation

**A** 音声を聞きながら、次の会話を読んでみましょう。  1-25 Audio

Sue: What time does the party start?

Jack: At 8 o'clock. Do you think we can still make it?

Sue: I think so, but driving in this ¹**gale** is pretty scary.

Jack: You're doing ²**fine**.

Sue: ³**Seriously**? Do you actually think so?

Jack: Absolutely. I ⁴**hate** driving in the rain.

Sue: I feel the same way. But it's the only way to get there in this weather.

Jack: Oh, did you feel that? Another gust of wind!

**B** Aの会話の太字部分の語句を下の語句と置きかえてペアで会話をしましょう。

| | | | |
|---|---|---|---|
| 1 | wind | storm | typhoon |
| 2 | really well | a great job | fantastically |
| 3 | Honestly | Truthfully | Really |
| 4 | dislike | detest | can't stand |

**C** ペアになって次の会話と同じ質問をしてみましょう。そして、例のように質問の回答を下の表に記入しましょう。

How do you feel about driving?

How do you get to school or work?

I like it, but I don't have a license.

I take the train.

| Partner's Name | How do you feel about driving? | Do you normally drive to school or work? |
|---|---|---|
| 1  Ken | *Like it, but no license* | *No–take the train* |
| 2 | | |
| 3 | | |
| 4 | | |

# Thinking About the Topic

次の意見に対して、自分が賛成なら agree に、反対なら disagree に☑をつけましょう。

1. A self-driving car with no driver may get lost.    ☑ agree   ☑ disagree

2. Self-driving cars are safer than other cars.    ☑ agree   ☑ disagree

3. I like driving so I will not use a self-driving car.    ☑ agree   ☑ disagree

4. In the future, all cars will be able to fly.    ☑ agree   ☑ disagree

5. I would like to drive a car underwater.    ☑ agree   ☑ disagree

# Talking About Your Idea

次の Discussion Starter の回答として自分の意見に近いほうを選び、その英文を完成させ、ペアかグループで発表しましょう。

| Discussion Starter | There are too many cars on the road. |
| --- | --- |

**Partner 1's Opinion**

> Using public transport is the best solution.

**Reasons to support my idea**

1. It is difficult to find a parking space _____.

2. Cars cost a lot of money _____.

3. Taking a train is less stressful than driving _____.

**Partner 2's Opinion**

> Car sharing is better than buying a car.

**Reasons to support my idea**

1. You do not need a garage _____.

2. Sharing saves money _____.

3. Driving less protects the environment _____.

# Organic Farming in Europe

## My Opinion

次の質問で自分の考えに合うものを選び、☑をつけましょう。

**1.** Generally speaking, organic food is healthier for you than non-organic food.

☑ agree ☑ not sure ☑ disagree

**2.** I am happy to pay more money for organic food products.

☑ agree ☑ not sure ☑ disagree

**3.** Organic farming is better for the environment than conventional farming.

☑ agree ☑ not sure ☑ disagree

# Vocabulary Refresh

次の文の空欄に適切な語句を右の囲みから選んで入れましょう。完成したら、音声を聞いて確認しましょう。

1. In recent years _____ has developed considerably among farmers and _____.

2. On _____, organic agriculture is estimated to cover some 58 million _____ of land.

3. There are three main _____ in organic farming.

4. Arable land crops include _____, _____ _____ and green fodder.

5. Some countries have lost _____ in the last 10 years.

6. More and more, people are filling their shopping bags with _____ _____.

**Vocabulary Box Items**

a global scale

cereals

consumers

crop types

fresh vegetables

hectares

organic farmland

organic produce

the organic sector

# First Watching

Video   1-27 Audio

**A** 次の写真のうち、動画の中で述べられている内容に近いほうを選び、☑をつけましょう。

**B** 次の文が動画の内容に対して正しければ True、誤まっていれば False に☑をつけましょう。

1. In 2017, almost half of the farmland in Europe was used for organic farming.  ☑ True  ☑ False

2. Fruit trees, olive groves and vineyards are given as examples of permanent crops.  ☑ True  ☑ False

3. Britain, Poland and Greece have the largest areas of organically-farmed land in the EU.  ☑ True  ☑ False

# Second Watching

**A** 次の英文は動画の内容を簡潔にまとめたものです。
もう一度動画を見る前にこの英文を読んで、音声を聞いてみましょう。

Since 1991, when the EU first started to regulate organic farming, the organic sector has developed considerably. In fact, by 2017, seven percent of land in Europe was organically farmed.

5　　Bulgaria, Croatia and France are still increasing their organic production, although countries like Poland and Greece have lost organic farmland.

Looking at the global picture, Europe now has the second largest area of organically-farmed land, 10　behind Oceania. Latin America is third.

In general, it still seems that more and more people are filling their shopping bags with organic produce.

**B** 次の文が動画の内容に対して正しければ True に、誤っていれば False に ☑ をつけましょう。

1. Labeling produce as organic started in the EU in 1991.　☑ True　☑ False

2. From 2012 to 2017, the area converted to organic production grew 50%.　☑ True　☑ False

3. Spain, Italy, France and Germany have the largest areas of organic farmland in the EU.　☑ True　☑ False

**C** 次の文は動画の内容に関するものです。誤りが含まれているので、その箇所を抜き出して修正してみましょう。

1. Oceania has the most organically-farmed land in the world, led by New Zealand.

➡

2. In 2017, the global market for organic produce was worth 34 billion euros.

➡

### stating intentions 意思を表明する

「〜するつもりである」という自分の意思を表すときには I intend to や I'm going to を使います。I'm planning to や I'm getting ready to も同じように使われますが、すでにそのための準備・計画を始めているといった意味合いが含まれます。目標を達成するために努力をしているという意味を込めるには、I aim to を使うのもいいでしょう。

- I'm going to be a teacher in the future. 「将来教師になるつもりです。」

- I intend to move out of my parents' house soon. 「もうすぐ実家を出るつもりです。」

- I'm planning to go abroad this summer. 「この夏は外国へ行く予定です。」

- I aim to improve my recipe. 「よりよいレシピにするために頑張っています。」

I want to を使って「〜したい」と希望を込めた意思を表すこともできます。really、definitely、desperately など副詞を伴ってその思いの強さを表すことができます。

- I desperately want to graduate. 「どうしても卒業したいのです。」

# Model Conversation

A 音声を聞きながら、次の会話を読んでみましょう。  1-29 Audio

Beth: I want to change the way I eat.

Derek: In what way?

Beth: I want to know more about healthy eating.

Derek: Do you have anything in mind?

Beth: I am ¹**planning** to take a cooking class.

Derek: ²**Cool**! Have you already decided what kind of class?

Beth: Not really. But I definitely want to cook ³**organic food**.

Derek: I can't wait to try it. That ⁴**Thai** dish you made was amazing!

**B** A の会話の太字部分の語句を下の語句と置きかえてペアで会話をしましょう。

| | | | |
|---|---|---|---|
| 1 | intending | getting ready | making plans |
| 2 | Good! | Great! | Fantastic! |
| 3 | food grown locally | fresh vegetables | natural food |
| 4 | Italian | Japanese | Korean |

**C** ペアになって次の会話と同じ質問をしてみましょう。そして、例のように質問の回答を下の表に記入しましょう。

Are you a healthy eater?

Is there anything you'd like to change about how you eat?

Yeah, most of the time.

Yes, I'd like to make my own lunch every day.

| Partner's Name | Are you a healthy eater? | Is there anything you'd like to change about how you eat? |
|---|---|---|
| 1　Emi | *most of the time* | *make my own lunch* |
| 2 | | |
| 3 | | |
| 4 | | |

# Thinking About the Topic

次の意見に対して、自分が賛成なら agree に、反対なら disagree に ☑ をつけましょう。

1. Organic food is expensive.          ☑ agree    ☑ disagree
2. Organic food is tastier than other food.    ☑ agree    ☑ disagree
3. I don't know much about organic farming.    ☑ agree    ☑ disagree
4. The things I eat are important to me.    ☑ agree    ☑ disagree
5. I prefer fast food.            ☑ agree    ☑ disagree

# Talking About Your Idea

次の Discussion Starter の回答として自分の意見に近いほうを選び、その英文を完成させ、ペアかグループで発表しましょう。

| **Discussion Starter** | Fast food is really popular. |
|---|---|

**Partner 1's Opinion**

Fast food matches my lifestyle.

**Reasons to support my idea**

1. It is sold everywhere _____.
2. It tastes really good _____.
3. It is cheap and convenient _____.

**Partner 2's Opinion**

I don't like to eat fast food often.

**Reasons to support my idea**

1. It is not organic _____.
2. We don't know what is in it _____.
3. The taste is not natural _____.

# Renewable Energy

## My Opinion

次の質問で自分の考えに合うものを選び、☑をつけましょう。

1. Japan should spend more money on developing wind and solar power.

   ☑ agree          ☑ not sure          ☑ disagree

2. All new houses and apartments should have solar panels.

   ☑ agree          ☑ not sure          ☑ disagree

3. In the future, most of our electricity will come from renewable energy sources.

   ☑ agree          ☑ not sure          ☑ disagree

# Vocabulary Refresh

次の文の空欄に適切な語句を右の囲みから選んで入れましょう。完成したら、音声を聞いて確認しましょう。

1. Offshore wind and _____ are seen as a crucial weapon in the fight against global warming.

2. Gas, _____ and oil are all _____ sources.

3. Battery technologies have been an _____ in the delivery of renewables-based electricity.

4. Renewables _____ double the amount of electricity produced by _____.

5. Technology improvements have played a _____ in increasing the amount of green energy produced.

6. The power and road transport _____ account for about half of _____ consumption.

**Vocabulary Box Items**

- coal
- conventional energy
- fossil fuel
- generate
- key role
- nuclear power
- obstacle
- sectors
- solar power

# First Watching

**A** 次の写真のうち、動画の中で述べられている内容に近いほうを選び、☑をつけましょう。

**B** 次の文が動画の内容に対して正しければ True、誤まっていれば False に ☑をつけましょう。

1. Green technologies are changing the way we produce energy. ☑True ☑False

2. It is very expensive to mass produce energy-saving batteries for electric vehicles. ☑True ☑False

3. Renewables' share of global energy consumption has increased five-fold since 2000. ☑True ☑False

# Second Watching

**A** 次の英文は動画の内容を簡潔にまとめたものです。
もう一度動画を見る前にこの英文を読んで、音声を聞いてみましょう。

1-32 Audio

Wind and solar power are changing the way we produce energy. And, unlike conventional energy sources, all countries have at least one source of renewable energy. The challenge is to develop
5  technologies and adapt to sometimes intermittent sources. No wind, for example, means no electricity.

But energy-saving batteries are already being mass-produced and residential energy storage technology could also become an attractive option
10  for homeowners.

Cheaper electric cars combined with renewable technology may stop growth in oil demand. However, even if solar and wind capacity continues to grow, scientists warn that it may not be fast enough to keep
15  global warming under control.

**B** 次の文が動画の内容に対して正しければ True に、誤っていれば False に ☑ をつけましょう。

1. Gas, coal and oil tend to be geographically concentrated.   ☑ True  ☑ False

2. Nuclear power is also seen as important in the fight against global warming.   ☑ True  ☑ False

3. Keeping global warming under 2°C was a goal of the 2015 Paris climate treaty.   ☑ True  ☑ False

**C** 次の文は動画の内容に関するものです。誤りが含まれているので、その箇所を抜き出して修正してみましょう。

1. Offshore wind and nuclear power are examples of what are called green technologies.

➡

2. Growth in the demand for renewables might be stopped from as early as 2020.

➡

### stating preferences　好みを述べる

英語では「どちらでもいい」という曖昧な態度はあまり歓迎されません。どちらが好みか聞かれたら、I like A better than B.、I prefer A to B.、I'd rather A（動詞）than B.、I choose A over B. などの表現を使って、できるだけはっきりと、どちらが好きか表明するようにしましょう。比べる対象が話の文脈から明らかなときは、than、to、over 以下を省略することも可能です。

- I definitely prefer butter <u>to</u> margarine.「私はマーガリンよりバターのほうが断然好き。」

- I'd rather have some extra time in bed <u>than</u> have breakfast.「朝食を食べるより少し長く寝ているほうがいい。」

- We always choose quality <u>over</u> quantity.「私たちは常に量より質を選びます。」

好みを表す形容詞（fond <u>of</u>、keen <u>on</u>）や名詞（<u>to</u> my taste/liking）を使って好みを表すこともできます。

- He's fond <u>of</u>/keen <u>on</u> baseball.「彼は野球が大好きだ／に夢中だ。」

- That movie was not really <u>to</u> my taste/liking.「あの映画はあまり私の好みではなかった。」

表現によって一緒に使われる前置詞が異なるので（下線部に注目）、それぞれセットで頭に入れておきましょう。

## Model Conversation

**A**　音声を聞きながら、次の会話を読んでみましょう。 🎧 1-33 Audio

Jodie: Do you like your new house better than the old one?

Fred: Sure, it's pretty cool! And my dad was really keen to move.

Jodie: Is that because he wanted more space?

Fred: No, not really. He preferred the solar roof on this house.

Jodie: Interesting! I guess that means you save money on [1]**electricity**.

Fred: Uh huh, that's the [2]**good thing**. The solar panels generate their own energy.

Jodie: So your parents made the [3]**right** choice then.

Fred: Yeah, [4]**especially** because we no longer have a leaking roof.

**B** **A** の会話の太字部分の語句を下の語句と置きかえてペアで会話をしましょう。

| 1 | power | your bills | household expenses |
|---|-------|------------|---------------------|
| 2 | advantage | bonus | appeal of it |
| 3 | correct | best | most sensible |
| 4 | in particular | largely | mainly |

**C** ペアになって次の会話と同じ質問をしてみましょう。そして、例のように質問の回答を下の表に記入しましょう。

Do you think carefully about the energy you use?

What can you do to save energy?

No, but I should.

I should use the stairs instead of the elevator.

| Partner's Name | Do you think carefully about the energy you use? | What can you do to save energy? |
|----------------|--------------------------------------------------|---------------------------------|
| 1   Gavin | *No, but I should.* | *use the stairs, not the elevator* |
| 2 | | |
| 3 | | |
| 4 | | |

# Thinking About the Topic

次の意見に対して、自分が賛成なら agree に、反対なら disagree に ☑をつけましょう。

1. Fossil fuels are necessary for a comfortable life.    ☑ agree   ☑ disagree
2. Using wind energy is cleaner than using oil.    ☑ agree   ☑ disagree
3. Buying oil and gas from other countries is expensive.    ☑ agree   ☑ disagree
4. We should build new nuclear power stations.    ☑ agree   ☑ disagree
5. Electric cars are cheap to run.    ☑ agree   ☑ disagree

# Talking About Your Idea

次の Discussion Starter の回答として自分の意見に近いほうを選び、その英文を完成させ、ペアかグループで発表しましょう。

| **Discussion Starter** | Using renewable energy will help to stop global warming. |
| --- | --- |

**Partner 1's Opinion**

Renewable energy is much cleaner than other energy.

**Reasons to support my idea**

1. Solar energy can be produced in our homes _____.
2. The wind is a free energy source _____.
3. There are no $CO_2$ emissions _____.

**Partner 2's Opinion**

We still depend on fossil fuels.

**Reasons to support my idea**

1. Gas is convenient for cooking _____.
2. Oil is needed to fuel airplane engines _____.
3. Cold countries use coal for heating _____.

# Whaling

## My Opinion

次の質問で自分の考えに合うものを選び、☑をつけましょう。

**1.** Killing whales for their meat is no different from killing cows for beef.

☑ agree          ☑ not sure          ☑ disagree

**2.** I would eat whale meat if I had the chance.

☑ agree          ☑ not sure          ☑ disagree

**3.** Keeping the oceans free of pollution is a more important issue than whaling.

☑ agree          ☑ not sure          ☑ disagree

# Vocabulary Refresh

次の文の空欄に適切な語句を右の囲みから選んで入れましょう。完成したら、音声を聞いて確認しましょう。

1. Entanglement in _____ is the biggest single threat to whales.

2. There is an international _____ on commercial whaling which _____ in 1986.

3. Aboriginal Subsistence Whaling is _____ and whales are taken by _____.

4. Japan says it only kills whales for the purposes of _____ _____.

5. The whaling industry is _____ and the demand for meat is falling.

6. Other threats to whales include oil exploration, _____ _____ and _____ supplies.

**Vocabulary Box Items**

- came into force
- diminishing food
- fishing gear
- in decline
- indigenous communities
- moratorium
- permitted
- polluted seas
- scientific research

# First Watching

Video  2-03 Audio

**A** 次の写真のうち、動画の中で述べられている内容に近いほうを選び、☑をつけましょう。

**B** 次の文が動画の内容に対して正しければ True、誤っていれば False に ☑をつけましょう。

1. There are around 90 species of whales, dolphins and porpoises worldwide.  ☑ True  ☑ False

2. The United Nations Whaling Community is the body which regulates whaling.  ☑ True  ☑ False

3. Indigenous communities in Greenland, Russia's Far East and Alaska continue to hunt whales.  ☑ True  ☑ False

# Second Watching

**A** 次の英文は動画の内容を簡潔にまとめたものです。
もう一度動画を見る前にこの英文を読んで、音声を聞いてみましょう。

2-04 Audio

Whales, dolphins and porpoises, known collectively as cetaceans, are among the planet's most endangered species.

Commercial whaling has largely stopped, but
5 hundreds of whales are still killed every year, mainly by Norway and Japan. Aboriginal Subsistence Whaling is also permitted, and 321 whales were taken by indigenous communities around the world in 2017.

Other threats to whale populations include oil
10 exploration, polluted seas and the loss of habitat.

But it's not all bad news. In 2016, most populations of humpback whale were taken off the United States endangered species list thanks to international conservation efforts.

＊ 2019 年 7 月、日本は IWC から
脱退し、商業捕鯨を再開した。

**B** 次の文が動画の内容に対して正しければ True に、誤っていれば False に ☑ をつけましょう。

1. Entanglement in fishing gear kills an estimated 300,000 whales, dolphins and porpoises every year. ☑ True ☑ False

2. Japan is the biggest hunter, netting some 432 minke whales in 2017. ☑ True ☑ False

3. In 2014, the UN's International Court of Justice allowed Tokyo to continue the Antarctic hunt. ☑ True ☑ False

**C** 次の文は動画の内容に関するものです。誤りが含まれているので、その箇所を抜き出して修正してみましょう。

1. Many types of whale were hunted around the world in the 20th century for meat and blubber.

➡

2. Opponents of whaling say it is inhumane, often subjecting whales to a long and stressful process.

➡

# Communication Focus

## checking understanding　理解を確認する

　コミュニケーションにおいて誤解の可能性はつきものですから、正しく理解しているかをその都度確認することが大事です。Do you mean ...? 「…という意味ですか？」、Do you want to ...? 「…したいのですか？」、Are you saying ...? 「…と言っているのですか？」などを使って、理解ができているかどうか確認しましょう。

- ■ Do you mean this Friday, or next Friday? 「今週の金曜日ですか、来週の金曜日ですか？」
- ■ Do you want to study abroad? 「留学したいのですか？」
- ■ Are you saying that he is lying? 「彼がウソをついているって言うの？」

　複雑な内容なら、Let me check if I understand well. 「ちゃんと理解しているかどうか確認させて。」とか Tell me if I'm wrong. 「間違っていたら言ってね。」などと前置きをしてから確認するのもいいでしょう。

　確認された側は、曖昧にせず That's correct. You're right. 「その通りです。」、That's not what I mean. 「そういう意味ではありません。」などはっきりと意図を表明し、説明を付け加えましょう。

# Model Conversation

**A**　音声を聞きながら、次の会話を読んでみましょう。

Sandra: Ready for the weekend trip?

Charlie: Yeah, just about. I've prepared all my fishing gear.

Sandra: Do you think we'll catch more than last time?

Charlie: ¹**Hopefully**! But do you want to catch more types of fish, or more fish in total?

Sandra: Both! We didn't get that many ²**before**.

Charlie: That's true, ³**but** we did get that one big fish.

Sandra: You're right, it was ⁴**a monster**!

Charlie: Let's hope we're lucky a second time.

**B** A の会話の太字部分の語句を下の語句と置きかえてペアで会話をしましょう。

| | | | |
|---|---|---|---|
| 1 | I hope so | All being well | With any luck |
| 2 | on that trip | previously | the last time |
| 3 | though | however | mind you |
| 4 | massive | enormous | gigantic |

**C** ペアになって次の会話と同じ質問をしてみましょう。そして、例のように質問の回答を下の表に記入しましょう。

Have you ever been fishing?

What do think about water sports?

Yes I have, but just once.

I love water polo!

| Partner's Name | | Have you ever been fishing? | What do think about water sports? |
|---|---|---|---|
| 1 | Nagi | *once* | *love water polo.* |
| 2 | | | |
| 3 | | | |
| 4 | | | |

# Thinking About the Topic

次の意見に対して、自分が賛成なら agree に、反対なら disagree に☑をつけましょう。

1. Dolphins are intelligent animals.   ☑ agree   ☑ disagree

2. Some people have to eat whales to survive.   ☑ agree   ☑ disagree

3. Whale meat is tastier than other kinds of meat.   ☑ agree   ☑ disagree

4. Fishing is a sport.   ☑ agree   ☑ disagree

5. Whales can communicate with other whales.   ☑ agree   ☑ disagree

# Talking About Your Idea

次の Discussion Starter の回答として自分の意見に近いほうを選び、その英文を完成させ、ペアかグループで発表しましょう。

| Discussion Starter | We should learn more about whales. |
| --- | --- |

**Partner 1's Opinion**

Whales are very important animals.

**Reasons to support my idea**

1. Whales support the ecosystem _____.

2. Whale watching is a popular tourist activity _____.

3. Whales sing to other whales _____.

**Partner 2's Opinion**

Some whaling is necessary.

**Reasons to support my idea**

1. Aboriginal Subsistence Whaling supports communities _____.

2. There is a long history of whaling _____.

3. Fishermen need jobs _____.

# Unit 10

# Air Pollution

## My Opinion

次の質問で自分の考えに合うものを選び、☑をつけましょう。

**1.** It is a good idea to wear a surgical mask to protect yourself from air pollution.

☑ agree                 ☑ not sure                ☑ disagree

**2.** The number of people suffering from breathing problems is increasing due to air pollution.

☑ agree                 ☑ not sure                ☑ disagree

**3.** We should make more effort to use electric vehicles in order to reduce air pollution.

☑ agree                 ☑ not sure                ☑ disagree

# Vocabulary Refresh

次の文の空欄に適切な語句を右の囲みから選んで入れましょう。完成したら、音声を聞いて確認しましょう。

1. Air pollution causes some seven million _____ _____ each year.

2. The very _____—released by fuels like _____—are the most dangerous.

3. Ozone exists naturally, but at ground level it's a _____ _____.

4. Ozone can damage vegetation and it causes stress for people with _____.

5. Nitrogen oxide reacts with _____ in the air to _____ _____ of nitric acid.

6. Pollutants can also affect the _____, eyes, _____ _____ or nervous system.

## Vocabulary Box Items

- asthma
- diesel
- digestive tract
- finest particles
- form a vapor
- health hazard
- lungs
- moisture
- premature deaths

# First Watching

**A** 次の写真のうち、動画の中で述べられている内容に近いほうを選び、☑をつけましょう。

**B** 次の文が動画の内容に対して正しければ True、誤まっていれば False に ☑をつけましょう。

1. More than a million children die each year because of air pollution. ☑ True ☑ False

2. Fine particles can be breathed into the lungs and enter the blood stream. ☑ True ☑ False

3. Ozone forms quickly in vehicle engines and power plants. ☑ True ☑ False

# Second Watching

**A** 次の英文は動画の内容を簡潔にまとめたものです。
もう一度動画を見る前にこの英文を読んで、音声を聞いてみましょう。　2-08 Audio

Seven million people, including a great many children, die each year because of air pollution.

Tiny particles are the most harmful form of air pollution. These are produced by farming, industry,
5 wood burners and road transport.

The smallest particles are the most dangerous. They enter the body through the lungs and get into the blood stream.

Ozone at ground level is also a pollutant. It
10 damages plants and causes stress for people with breathing problems.

Another dangerous gas, nitrogen oxide, is produced by engines and power plants. Reacting with moisture in the air to form nitric acid, it worsens a
15 number of health problems.

**B** 次の文が動画の内容に対して正しければ True に、誤っていれば False に ☑ をつけましょう。

1. Many different pollutants exist in the air.      ☑ True    ☑ False

2. Microscopic particles are only produced by farming and wood burners.    ☑ True    ☑ False

3. Sulphur dioxide, benzene and ammonia are given as examples of pollutants.    ☑ True    ☑ False

**C** 次の文は動画の内容に関するものです。誤りが含まれているので、その箇所を抜き出して修正してみましょう。

1. Ozone is created by chemical reactions in the presence of water.

 →

2. Nitric acid can worsen bronchitis and other breathing diseases.

 →

## giving reasons 理由を述べる

「なぜ」「なにが原因で」などと聞かれた場合に理由を説明しますが、because の誤用・多用には気をつけましょう。特に because の節だけを単独で使うのは避けましょう。

■ A:You look tired. What's wrong? 「疲れているみたいね。どうしたの?」

△ B: Because I stayed up late last night. 「昨晩は夜更かししたんだ。」 (**O** It's because ….)

**O** B: Yeah, I'm tired because I've been busy recently. 「うん、最近忙しくて疲れているんだ。」

理由を述べるには、話し言葉では特に so もよく使われます。

■ I stayed up late, so I'm tired. ＝ I'm tired because I stayed up late.

ただし、理由を言うときに So で文を始めることはできません。

✘ So I couldn't sleep well last night. 「昨夜はよく眠れなかったから…」

**O** I had bad dreams last night, so I'm tired. 「夜、悪い夢を見たから疲れている。」

はっきりと理由を聞かれている場面では、because や so なしで理由を述べても不自然ではありません。

■ A: Why didn't you answer my call last night? 「なんで昨晩は電話に出なかったの?」

B: Oh, I was already in bed by 10. 「あー、10 時にはもう寝ていたわ。」

# Model Conversation

A 音声を聞きながら、次の会話を読んでみましょう。 2-09 Audio

Stacy: Hey Jed, can you help me with my ¹**homework**?

Jed: I can try. What is it?

Stacy: I have to explain the danger of air pollution for my ²**science** class.

Jed: OK, let me think. Pollution harms us when we breathe in dust.

Stacy: Er, what kind of dust?

Jed: Like the dust that comes from ³**industry**.

Stacy: So what exactly is the problem with dust?

Jed: The particles are often ⁴**tiny**, so they easily enter our lungs and harm us.

**B** Ａ の会話の太字部分の語句を下の語句と置きかえてペアで会話をしましょう。

| | | | |
|---|---|---|---|
| 1 | assignment | schoolwork | report |
| 2 | social studies | environmental science | biology |
| 3 | factories | cities | big buildings |
| 4 | really small | minuscule | minute |

**C** ペアになって次の会話と同じ質問をしてみましょう。そして、例のように質問の回答を下の表に記入しましょう。

Is there any pollution where you live?

Do you prefer the city or the countryside?

Yes, noise pollution because I live next to a busy road.

I prefer the countryside because it's quieter.

| Partner's Name | Is there any pollution where you live? | Do you prefer the city or the countryside? |
|---|---|---|
| 1   Sophie | *Yes, noise—busy road* | *Countryside—quieter* |
| 2 | | |
| 3 | | |
| 4 | | |

# Thinking About the Topic

次の意見に対して、自分が賛成なら agree に、反対なら disagree に☑をつけましょう。

1. There are many kinds of pollution.    ☑ agree    ☑ disagree

2. Driving cars is bad for the air.    ☑ agree    ☑ disagree

3. Cities are dirtier than the countryside.    ☑ agree    ☑ disagree

4. Air pollution is dangerous for people's health.    ☑ agree    ☑ disagree

5. There are things we can do to improve the quality of the air.    ☑ agree    ☑ disagree

# Talking About Your Idea

次の Discussion Starter の回答として自分の意見に近いほうを選び、その英文を完成させ、ペアかグループで発表しましょう。

| **Discussion Starter** | The air is better in the countryside than in the city. |
| --- | --- |

**Partner 1's Opinion**

It's true that cities have bad air.

### Reasons to support my idea

1. Cities are crowded _____.

2. There are too many cars and buses _____.

3. Many big factories are in cities _____.

**Partner 2's Opinion**

Actually, I prefer living in the city.

### Reasons to support my idea

1. Buses and trains are really convenient _____.

2. Cities are exciting for young people _____.

3. We can grow more trees and clean up cities _____.

# Facial Recognition

## My Opinion

次の質問で自分の考えに合うものを選び、☑をつけましょう。

**1.** I often have trouble remembering my passwords.

☑ agree              ☑ not sure              ☑ disagree

**2.** Facial recognition is safer than using a password to identify yourself.

☑ agree              ☑ not sure              ☑ disagree

**3.** I think facial recognition is a threat to privacy.

☑ agree              ☑ not sure              ☑ disagree

# Vocabulary Refresh

次の文の空欄に適切な語句を右の囲みから選んで入れましょう。完成したら、音声を聞いて確認しましょう。

1. Facial recognition is a technology used to _____ or identify an individual from a photograph.

2. The technique makes it possible to check that _____ is who he or she claims to be.

3. Software _____ an image based on a face's _____.

4. The next step is to compare the face print with images in a _____.

5. Facial recognition is now used to access _____ and _____ platforms.

6. Facial recognition could also present a threat to _____ and _____.

**Vocabulary Box Items**

- an individual
- individual liberties
- bank accounts
- database
- unique traits
- social media
- authenticate
- privacy
- generates

# First Watching

Video | 2-11 Audio

**A** 次の写真のうち、動画の中で述べられている内容に近いほうを選び、☑をつけましょう。

**B** 次の文が動画の内容に対して正しければ True、誤っていれば False に☑をつけましょう。

1. Facial recognition is a biometric technology. ☑ True ☑ False

2. Facial recognition takes a person's hair into account. ☑ True ☑ False

3. Facial recognition was originally used to fight crime. ☑ True ☑ False

# Second Watching

**A** 次の英文は動画の内容を簡潔にまとめたものです。
もう一度動画を見る前にこの英文を読んで、音声を聞いてみましょう。

2-12 Audio

Facial recognition is used to identify an individual from a photograph or facial image. This makes it possible to check that an individual is who he or she claims to be.

5　From a photograph or from video, software creates an image based on a face's unique traits. It then compares the image with images in a database.

Facial recognition was originally used to
10　fight crime, but now has everyday uses such as accessing social media.

However, some people don't like it. They think that facial recognition technology threatens their privacy and have questions about how databases
15　are used.

**B** 次の文が動画の内容に対して正しければ True に、誤っていれば False に ☑ をつけましょう。

1. Facial recognition can't identify an individual in a group.　　☑ True　☑ False

2. The shape of the nose, eyebrows, and mouth are some of a face's unique traits.　☑ True　☑ False

3. Facial recognition has largely failed at fighting crime.　　☑ True　☑ False

**C** 次の文は動画の内容に関するものです。誤りが含まれているので、その箇所を抜き出して修正してみましょう。

1. Hair and clothes are not taken into databases by facial recognition technology.

➡

2. To reduce the margin of error, the quality of the face must be good.

➡

# Communication Focus

## making suggestions 提案する

　人がどうしたらいいかと思案しているときに「〜してみたら?」と提案する場合は、押しつけがましくないのがいいと思うかもしれませんが、砕けた会話ならストレートに命令形で言っても強すぎることはありません。特に try と一緒に使うといいでしょう。

　それでも直接的になりすぎると思うなら、How about ...?、I suggest/recommend V+ing/that ... を使うといいでしょう。suggest や recommend のあとに that 節(that は省略可能)を続けるときには、動詞の原形あるいは should +原形が来ることに注意してください。

> ■ I don't know what to say to my sister. She is so nervous.
> 　「妹がすごく緊張してて…なんと言ってあげたらいいのか分からない。」
>> ➡ Just tell her to relax. 「リラックスしてって言ってあげて。」
>> ➡ Try convincing her that she can do it. 「君ならできるって言い聞かせてみて。」
>> ➡ How about telling her a joke? 「冗談でも言ってみたら。」
>> ➡ I'd suggest (that) she (should) take a deep breath. 「私なら深呼吸をするように言うよ。」

　提案や助言の場面で had better「〜するのがいい」を使うのは、上の立場から言われている感じを与えかねないので、控えたほうがいいでしょう。ただし、Oops! I'd better hurry up. 「わー、急がなくちゃ。」のように、自分がなにかしたほうがいいときに使うのは構いません。

# Model Conversation

A 音声を聞きながら、次の会話を読んでみましょう。  2-13 Audio

Liz: My mom says she's worried about all the cameras filming her in town.

Dave: Tell her to relax, they don't do anything.

Liz: I tried that. It didn't work.

Dave: Then try explaining that they are not interested in her.

Liz: Hmm. That might work. The problem is, she is concerned about her **¹privacy**.

Dave: Well, how about showing her the positive **²side** of them?

Liz: But is there anything good **³about** facial recognition?

Dave: **⁴Oh yeah**! It keeps us safe from criminals.

**B** Aの会話の太字部分の語句を下の語句と置きかえてペアで会話をしましょう。

| | | | |
|---|---|---|---|
| 1 | individual liberties | freedom | rights |
| 2 | aspect | part | features |
| 3 | regarding | concerning | with regard to |
| 4 | Obviously | Clearly | Of course |

**C** ペアになって次の会話と同じ質問をしてみましょう。そして、例のように質問の回答を下の表に記入しましょう。

Are you worried about cameras spying on you?

Is there any security feature you really like?

Yes, but not so much.

I love the fingerprint ID on my phone.

| Partner's Name | Are you worried about cameras spying on you? | Is there any security feature you really like? |
|---|---|---|
| 1   Saki | *Yes–a little* | *fingerprint ID on my phone* |
| 2 | | |
| 3 | | |
| 4 | | |

# Thinking About the Topic

次の意見に対して、自分が賛成なら agree に、反対なら disagree に ☑ をつけましょう。

1. I have to remember too many passwords.　　　　　　　　　　　　　　☑ agree　☑ disagree

2. Facial recognition is a great feature for phones and computers.　　☑ agree　☑ disagree

3. Cameras do not make the streets any safer.　　　　　　　　　　　☑ agree　☑ disagree

4. My privacy is very important to me.　　　　　　　　　　　　　　☑ agree　☑ disagree

5. Only criminals are worried about being filmed in public.　　　　　☑ agree　☑ disagree

# Talking About Your Idea

次の Discussion Starter の回答として自分の意見に近いほうを選び、その英文を完成させ、ペアかグループで発表しましょう。

| **Discussion Starter** | Facial recognition is making the world much safer. |
| --- | --- |

**Partner 1's Opinion**

It is easier for the police to catch criminals.

**Reasons to support my idea**

1. Cameras can find criminals anywhere _____.

2. Fake IDs will not work _____.

3. We will not need so many police on the streets _____.

**Partner 2's Opinion**

There are still several dangers.

**Reasons to support my idea**

1. My individual liberties are at risk _____.

2. Anyone can spy on us _____.

3. Criminals may use new technology in bad ways _____.

74

# Food Waste

## My Opinion

次の質問で自分の考えに合うものを選び、☑をつけましょう。

**1.** I often throw old and uneaten fruit and vegetables in the trash.

☑ agree ☑ not sure ☑ disagree

**2.** Supermarkets should give away the food they can't sell to the poor.

☑ agree ☑ not sure ☑ disagree

**3.** People should take uneaten food home with them from restaurants.

☑ agree ☑ not sure ☑ disagree

# Vocabulary Refresh

次の文の空欄に適切な語句を右の囲みから選んで入れましょう。完成したら、音声を聞いて確認しましょう。 🎧 2-14 Audio

1. Throwing away food meant for _____ is a _____ of money.

2. Fruit and vegetables, fish, eggs and milk are all _____ thrown away.

3. Waste can occur during food production, _____, _____ or consumption.

4. Producers are being advised to _____ to avoid _____.

5. Consumers are being _____ to buy less food.

6. Asking for a _____ after eating out is _____ in many countries.

**Vocabulary Box Items**

- commonly
- commonplace
- cooperate
- distribution
- doggy bag
- human consumption
- massive waste
- overproduction
- storage
- urged

# First Watching  🖥 Video  🎧 2-15 Audio

**A** 次の写真のうち、動画の中で述べられている内容に近いほうを選び、☑をつけましょう。

a ☑

b ☑

**B** 次の文が動画の内容に対して正しければ True、誤まっていれば False に☑をつけましょう。

1. Every six months 1.3 billion tons of food intended for humans is wasted.   ☑ True   ☑ False

2. In developing countries, wastage mainly occurs during distribution and consumption.   ☑ True   ☑ False

3. Awareness campaigns are trying to highlight the issue of food waste.   ☑ True   ☑ False

76

# Second Watching

**A** 次の英文は動画の内容を簡潔にまとめたものです。
もう一度動画を見る前にこの英文を読んで、音声を聞いてみましょう。

Each year, enough food to feed much of the world's population is wasted. This is not only a waste of food, but is also a massive waste of money and water. Most commonly thrown away are fruit and
5  vegetables, fish, cereals, eggs and milk.

In developing countries, food waste usually occurs during production and storage. However, in rich countries, wastage is greater during distribution and consumption.
10  Campaigners are advising food producers to avoid overproduction and build more storage facilities. Consumers meanwhile are being urged to buy less.

**B** 次の文が動画の内容に対して正しければ True に、誤っていれば False に ☑ をつけましょう。

1. The food wasted every year is enough to feed Africa, Europe and the Americas.   ☑ True   ☑ False

2. The food wasted every year equals more than $100 billion simply thrown away.   ☑ True   ☑ False

3. Food producers are being urged to sell directly to the public rather than through supermarkets.   ☑ True   ☑ False

**C** 次の文は動画の内容に関するものです。誤りが含まれているので、その箇所を抜き出して修正してみましょう。

1. The reason why so much food is wasted varies by religion.

→

2. As well as being asked to buy less, consumers are being urged to grow food.

→

## Communication Focus

### offering to do something　手助けを申し出る

　困っている人を助けようと申し出るときには、相手がその申し出を受け入れるのが負担になりすぎないように少し控えめに、でも助けたい気持ちをはっきりと表す必要があります。help を使うとやや直接的ですが、意図は明確です。

- Can I help you?「お手伝いしましょうか?」 / How can I help?「何かお手伝いできますか?」

help ではなく can do (for you) を使うと少し控えめな感じを出すことができます。手助けしたい気持ちを明確にするためには、これらの文の後に、I want to help.「お役に立ちたいのです」と添えてもいいでしょう。

- Is there anything I can do? / What can I do for you?「何か私にできることはありますか?」

- Tell me what I can do. / Can you tell me what I can do?「何ができるか教えてください。」

申し出を受け入れる側も、Really?「ほんとうですか?」 Can you? It'd be great.「(手伝ってもらえるなら) すばらしい。」などのように感謝の気持ちを明確に表します。同時に、直接的になりすぎないように、何をしてもらいたいのか控えめに依頼しましょう。

- I'd be grateful if you could ....「〜してもらえるとしたらありがたい。」

- Do you think you could …?「〜してもらえるかしら?」

## Model Conversation

A　音声を聞きながら、次の会話を読んでみましょう。  2-17 Audio

Clare: Do you remember my ¹**friend** Junko?

Mike: I think so…

Clare: She's trying to collect food for a food bank.

Mike: Oh yeah, I remember. It must be ²**a lot** of work.

Clare: She really needs more volunteers.

Mike: Is there anything I can do? I have some free time.

Clare: Really? Do you think you could ³**cooperate**? She'd be so grateful.

Mike: I'd be ⁴**happy** to.

**B** **A** の会話の太字部分の語句を下の語句と置きかえてペアで会話をしましょう。

| | | | |
|---|---|---|---|
| 1 | cousin | classmate | coworker |
| 2 | plenty | tons | loads |
| 3 | lend a hand | help out | assist |
| 4 | glad | pleased | delighted |

**C** ペアになって次の会話と同じ質問をしてみましょう。そして、例のように質問の回答を下の表に記入しましょう。

Do you always eat everything on your plate?

Is there anything you don't eat?

I try to.

Well, I don't eat snails.

| Partner's Name | Do you always eat everything on your plate? | Is there anything you don't eat? |
|---|---|---|
| 1     Bob | *I try to.* | *snails* |
| 2 | | |
| 3 | | |
| 4 | | |

# Thinking About the Topic

次の意見に対して、自分が賛成なら agree に、反対なら disagree に ☑ をつけましょう。

1. Many people waste food in their homes.    ☑ agree   ☑ disagree

2. My school has a good choice of food to buy for lunch.    ☑ agree   ☑ disagree

3. Everyone on the planet has enough to eat.    ☑ agree   ☑ disagree

4. I never ask for a doggy bag in a restaurant.    ☑ agree   ☑ disagree

5. Supermarkets and restaurants do not throw food away.    ☑ agree   ☑ disagree

# Talking About Your Idea

次の Discussion Starter の回答として自分の意見に近いほうを選び、その英文を完成させ、ペアかグループで発表しましょう。

| **Discussion Starter** | We need to stop wasting so much food. |
|---|---|

**Partner 1's Opinion**

> Everybody wastes some food.

Reasons to support my idea

1. I don't want to eat food that's not fresh _____ .

2. Sometimes restaurants serve me too much food _____ .

3. I have to throw old food away _____ .

**Partner 2's Opinion**

> There are some things I do to stop wasting food.

**Reasons to support my idea**

1. I get a doggy bag _____ .

2. I freeze extra food _____ .

3. I eat fruit that isn't perfect _____ .

# Voyager, the Solar System and Beyond

## My Opinion

次の質問で自分の考えに合うものを選び、☑をつけましょう。

1. Governments should spend much more money on exploring space.

   ☑ agree        ☑ not sure        ☑ disagree

2. Earth cannot be the only place in the universe which contains life.

   ☑ agree        ☑ not sure        ☑ disagree

3. Human beings will one day be able to travel to other stars and solar systems.

   ☑ agree        ☑ not sure        ☑ disagree

# Vocabulary Refresh

次の文の空欄に適切な語句を右の囲みから選んで入れましょう。完成したら、音声を聞いて確認しましょう。

1. Voyagers 1 and 2 were _____ on a mission _____ the solar system.

2. The spacecraft soon moved on to the two outermost _____ _____, Uranus and Neptune.

3. Each spacecraft carries _____ in case of a chance encounter with _____.

4. Signals _____ to Earth are sent with the power of just 20 _____.

5. Voyager 2, traveling south, entered _____ at the end of 2018.

6. All the spacecraft's _____ will have _____ _____ permanently in 2030.

**Vocabulary Box Items**

- a time capsule
- beamed
- extra-terrestrials
- giant planets
- instruments
- interstellar space
- launched
- to explore
- to shut down
- watts

# First Watching  Video  2-19 Audio

**A** 次の写真のうち、動画の中で述べられている内容に近いほうを選び、☑をつけましょう。

a

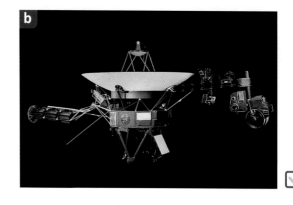
b

**B** 次の文が動画の内容に対して正しければ True、誤まっていれば False に ☑をつけましょう。

1. The original aim of Voyagers 1 and 2 was to concentrate on Uranus and Neptune. ☑ True ☑ False

2. It is a journey of billions of kilometers from Earth to the outer reaches of the Solar System. ☑ True ☑ False

3. The two spacecraft may continue to wander through space for billions of years. ☑ True ☑ False

# Second Watching

A 次の英文は動画の内容を簡潔にまとめたものです。
もう一度動画を見る前にこの英文を読んで、音声を聞いてみましょう。

> Voyagers 1 and 2 were launched in 1977 to explore the solar system.
>
> They originally concentrated on Jupiter and Saturn, but the spacecraft soon moved on to the
> 5  outer reaches of the Solar System.
>
> The spacecraft both carry a time capsule in case of an encounter with extra-terrestrials. They are also fitted with television cameras and various sensors.
>
> In 2012 Voyager 1 left the solar system. It was
> 10  followed by Voyager 2, which entered interstellar space in 2018.
>
> Although their instruments will shut down in 2030, the two spacecraft may continue to travel through space for billions of years.

B 次の文が動画の内容に対して正しければ True に、誤っていれば False に ☑ をつけましょう。

1. Voyager 1 and Voyager 2 are exactly the same. ☑ True ☑ False

2. The time capsule is a gold box containing photographs of life on Earth. ☑ True ☑ False

3. Neither spacecraft is expected to come into contact with another star for over 40,000 years. ☑ True ☑ False

C 次の文は動画の内容に関するものです。誤りが含まれているので、その箇所を抜き出して修正してみましょう。

1. Voyager 1 became the first spacecraft to lose contact with Earth when it passed outside the heliosphere.

➡

2. The heliosphere is a bubble-like region that extends about 30 million kilometers beyond all the planets.

➡

# Communication Focus

## persuading　説得する

　宇宙人は存在するかどうかという壮大な議論に限らず、人を説得して同意してもらうことや、納得して何かをしてもらうことはよくあります。その際には、まずは自分がそのテーマに強く確信を持っている意思表示をし、相手に信頼してもらえるような理由を挙げます。Believe me. や Trust me. など、「私を信じて。」と付け加えてもいいでしょう。

■ A: I don't know if I want to go to the party tonight. 「今夜のパーティーにあまり行きたくないかも。」

　B: I'm sure it'll be fun. A lot of people who you haven't seen for a while will come. Trust me. You'll enjoy it. 「きっと楽しいよ。長いこと会っていない人達が来るよ。信じて。絶対楽しめるって。」

　A: Yeah, you may be right. 「たしかにそうかもね。」

　説得される側は相手の説得に対して、同意できないなら、その意思を伝えることが大切です。No! と完全否定する必要はなく、多少の理解を示した上で、躊躇を表したほうが無難でしょう。

■ I'm not sure. 「どうかしら。」

■ I'm still not convinced. 「うーん、まだよく分からないわ。」

■ I agree with you to some extent, but … 「ある程度分かるけど…」

# Model Conversation

**A**　音声を聞きながら、次の会話を読んでみましょう。  2-21 Audio

Sid: I'm certain there is extra-terrestrial life. You know, aliens.

Nancy: What? You're kidding! How can you be so sure?

Sid: Well, one reason is because we know there are other planets.

Nancy: OK, that I can understand.

Sid: And secondly, there are [1]**frequent** sightings of UFOs.

Nancy: I've heard about them too, but I'm not [2]**convinced**.

Sid: Then how do you explain all the other [3]**evidence**?

Nancy: I can't. I guess I agree with you [4]**up to a point**.

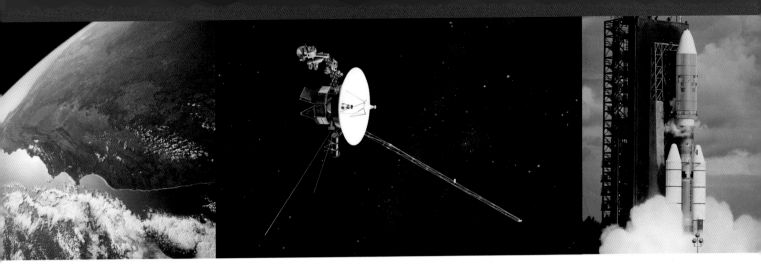

**B** **A** の会話の太字部分の語句を下の語句と置きかえてペアで会話をしましょう。

| | | | |
|---|---|---|---|
| 1 | regular | many | numerous |
| 2 | persuaded | certain | sure |
| 3 | facts | signs | reports |
| 4 | partly | to some extent | to a certain degree |

**C** ペアになって次の会話と同じ質問をしてみましょう。そして、例のように質問の回答を下の表に記入しましょう。

Would you like to travel into space?

Yeah, it must be beautiful.

Have you ever seen a UFO?

Of course not!

| Partner's Name | Would you like to travel into space? | Have you ever seen a UFO? |
|---|---|---|
| 1   Megan | *Yes–beautiful* | *Of course not!* |
| 2 | | |
| 3 | | |
| 4 | | |

# Thinking About the Topic

次の意見に対して、自分が賛成なら agree に、反対なら disagree に☑をつけましょう。

1. Space travel is becoming easier.    ☑ agree   ☑ disagree

2. There is certainly life on other planets.    ☑ agree   ☑ disagree

3. In the future, humans will travel at the speed of light.    ☑ agree   ☑ disagree

4. We will live on Mars in about 100 years' time.    ☑ agree   ☑ disagree

5. Aliens are going to attack Earth.    ☑ agree   ☑ disagree

# Talking About Your Idea

次の Discussion Starter の回答として自分の意見に近いほうを選び、その英文を完成させ、ペアかグループで発表しましょう。

| **Discussion Starter** | The human race will live in space in the future. |
|---|---|

**Partner 1's Opinion**

Earth has too many problems.

Reasons to support my idea

1. There are too many people _____.

2. The air is polluted _____.

3. There is not enough clean water _____.

**Partner 2's Opinion**

Space travel has many advantages.

Reasons to support my idea

1. We can explore new planets _____.

2. There is no problem of gravity on Mars _____.

3. Travel will be cheaper, easier and faster _____.

# Ocean Garbage

## My Opinion

次の質問で自分の考えに合うものを選び、☑をつけましょう。

1. Keeping the oceans free of pollution is one of the most important problems facing humanity.

   ☑ agree        ☑ not sure        ☑ disagree

2. Stopping people using plastic products in their daily lives is impossible.

   ☑ agree        ☑ not sure        ☑ disagree

3. People should always have to pay for plastic items like bags and straws.

   ☑ agree        ☑ not sure        ☑ disagree

# Vocabulary Refresh

次の文の空欄に適切な語句を右の囲みから選んで入れましょう。完成したら、音声を聞いて確認しましょう。

1. The Great Pacific Garbage Patch is a plastic soup of _____ bags and bottles.

2. The earth's oceans hold millions of tons of _____ _____, which can be _____ deep.

3. Some _____ mistake plastic for food and harm their _____.

4. A wingless _____ threatens the balance of _____.

5. The Mediterranean Sea is _____ with tiny pieces of floating debris.

6. Some plastics can take more than 100 years _____.

### Vocabulary Box Items

- digestive systems
- discarded
- marine mammals
- oceanic ecosystems
- polluted
- polluting debris
- scores of meters
- to degrade
- water insect

# First Watching

**A** 次の写真のうち、動画の中で述べられている内容に近いほうを選び、☑をつけましょう。

**B** 次の文が動画の内容に対して正しければ True、誤まっていれば False に☑をつけましょう。

1. The Great Pacific Garbage Patch is bigger than France, Germany and Spain combined. ☑ True ☑ False

2. The Great Pacific Garbage Patch is a hundred times bigger than 40 years ago. ☑ True ☑ False

3. The Great Pacific Garbage Patch is located between Hawaii and Japan. ☑ True ☑ False

# Second Watching

 Video   2-23 Audio

**A** 次の英文は動画の内容を簡潔にまとめたものです。
もう一度動画を見る前にこの英文を読んで、音声を聞いてみましょう。

2-24 Audio

> The Great Pacific Garbage Patch is a huge and growing mass of plastic and other waste in the Pacific Ocean. This waste floats on the surface of the ocean and in some places is meters
> 5 deep.
> Marine creatures can mistake plastic for food and eat it. This harms their health. Additionally, the garbage is a breeding ground for a water insect which threatens the balance of oceanic
> 10 ecosystems.
> The most polluted sea is the Mediterranean. It contains billions of tiny pieces of floating rubbish. Almost enclosed by land, its waters need about 90 years to clean and renew themselves.

**B** 次の文が動画の内容に対して正しければ True に、誤っていれば False に ☑ をつけましょう。

1. The Great Pacific Garbage Patch is closest to the country of Chile.　☑ True　☑ False

2. Four other oceans also hold millions of tons of polluting debris.　☑ True　☑ False

3. The highest average density of plastic can be found in the Indian Ocean.　☑ True　☑ False

**C** 次の文は動画の内容に関するものです。誤りが含まれているので、その箇所を抜き出して修正してみましょう。

1. A wingless water insect, the Halobates sericeus, can be found in the South Atlantic.

> ➡

2. The Mediterranean Sea contains about 150 million tiny pieces of floating rubbish.

> ➡

## Communication Focus

### asking for information / giving information 質問する・答える

何か情報が欲しいとき、人は質問をします。疑問文を使うのが一番シンプルな方法ですが、それ以外にも付加疑問文や命令文で情報を求めることも出来ます。

- ■ **疑問文**：Is it a big problem?「それは大きな問題なの?」
- ■ **付加疑問文**：We can fix the problem, can't we?「問題は解決できるんでしょう?」
- ■ **命令文**：Tell me how serious the problem is.「問題がどれだけ深刻なのか教えて。」

また、唐突に質問をするのではなく、質問する理由を先に述べたり、垣根表現（hedge）や語調を和らげる言葉（I guess、I wonder など）を付けたりする工夫もしましょう。What time is she coming back?「彼女は何時に帰ってくるの?」と聞くより、Do you know what time she is coming back?「彼女は何時に帰ってくるのか分かる?」と聞いたほうが、ぶしつけにならずに済みます。

答える側も断言しすぎないように、同じように hedge を使って話します（I'm sorry to tell you but ...、As you know...、Well, ... など）。情報をもらった側はそれに対して驚きや落胆などの受け止めを大きく表現するといいでしょう。Wow!、Great!、What?!、Really?、No way!、Oh my god! などの表現があります。

## Model Conversation

**A** 音声を聞きながら、次の会話を読んでみましょう。 2-25 Audio

Shawn: On the news they were talking about garbage in the ocean.

Lisa: It's a big topic right now.

Shawn: I know you study this, Lisa. So, just how big is the problem?

Lisa: Well, it is extremely serious.
There has been a lot of damage to [1]**the ecosystem**.

Shawn: Gosh! I [2]**guess** we can do something, can't we?

Lisa: Sure, we can find [3]**a solution** if we change our behavior.

Shawn: Do you really [4]**imagine** people will change?

Lisa: Hmm. I am pretty sure we have no choice.

**B** Aの会話の太字部分の語句を下の語句と置きかえてペアで会話をしましょう。

| | | | |
|---|---|---|---|
| **1** | the oceans | marine mammals | lakes and rivers |
| **2** | reckon | figure | suppose |
| **3** | an answer | a fix | a way out |
| **4** | think | believe | suppose |

**C** ペアになって次の会話と同じ質問をしてみましょう。そして、例のように質問の回答を下の表に記入しましょう。

What do you like about the sea?

How should we keep the oceans clean?

I like the smell of sea air.

We should always take our trash home.

| Partner's Name | What do you like about the sea? | How should we keep the oceans clean? |
|---|---|---|
| 1 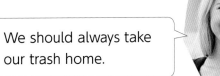 Kim | *the sea air* | *take our trash home* |
| 2 | | |
| 3 | | |
| 4 | | |

# Thinking About the Topic

次の意見に対して、自分が賛成なら agree に、反対なら disagree に☑をつけましょう。

1. The oceans should be cleaner.　　　　　　　　　　　☑ agree　　☑ disagree

2. There is nothing I can do to help clean the oceans.　☑ agree　　☑ disagree

3. Technology will solve the garbage problem.　　　　　☑ agree　　☑ disagree

4. I probably use too much plastic.　　　　　　　　　☑ agree　　☑ disagree

5. People need clean water to live.　　　　　　　　　☑ agree　　☑ disagree

# Talking About Your Idea

次の Discussion Starter の回答として自分の意見に近いほうを選び、その英文を完成させ、ペアかグループで発表しましょう。

| **Discussion Starter** | Clean water is very important. |
|---|---|

**Partner 1's Opinion**

We depend on clean water to live.

Reasons to support my idea

1. We use water for drinking _____.

2. Water is necessary for washing _____.

3. Many kinds of animals live in water _____.

**Partner 2's Opinion**

Dirty water causes many problems.

Reasons to support my idea

1. The oceans are polluted _____.

2. Fish eat plastic _____.

3. We can catch diseases from water _____.

# Planned Obsolescence

## My Opinion

次の質問で自分の考えに合うものを選び、☑をつけましょう。

**1.** I like to replace my smartphone every one or two years.

  ☑ agree  ☑ not sure  ☑ disagree

**2.** It would be more environmentally friendly if products were made to last longer.

  ☑ agree  ☑ not sure  ☑ disagree

**3.** Planned obsolescence should be an illegal industrial strategy.

  ☑ agree  ☑ not sure  ☑ disagree

# Vocabulary Refresh

次の文の空欄に適切な語句を右の囲みから選んで入れましょう。完成したら、音声を聞いて確認しましょう。

1. Planned obsolescence is a _____ used by manufacturers to limit the _____ of their products.

2. Planned obsolescence encourages customers to _____ _____ frequently.

3. Consumers change their smartphone because an _____ _____ appears _____.

4. Seven billion smartphones have been sold _____ since 2007, and this hasn't been without _____.

5. What should be done with the electronic and _____ _____ generated around the world?

6. It is difficult to prove _____ as an industrial strategy.

**Vocabulary Box Items**

- electrical waste
- improved version
- life span
- on the market
- planned obsolescence
- ramifications
- replace items
- strategy
- worldwide

# First Watching

Video | 2-27 Audio

**A** 次の写真のうち、動画の中で述べられている内容に近いほうを選び、☑をつけましょう。

**B** 次の文が動画の内容に対して正しければ True、誤まっていれば False に ☑をつけましょう。

1. The phrase planned obsolescence was first used in Europe in 1932. ☑ True ☑ False

2. Screen manufacturing causes global warming due to toxic discharges. ☑ True ☑ False

3. Only 20% of electronic and electrical waste is recycled. ☑ True ☑ False

# Second Watching

**A** 次の英文は動画の内容を簡潔にまとめたものです。
もう一度動画を見る前にこの英文を読んで、音声を聞いてみましょう。

2-28 Audio

Planned obsolescence is not new. It was first suggested in 1932 as a way to stimulate industry and growth.

Planned obsolescence is a strategy used by
5 manufacturers to limit the life span of products so that they are frequently replaced. For example, consumers often change their smartphone when an improved version appears.

The frequent buying of new products generated 44.7
10 million tons of electronic and electrical waste in 2016. Some of this waste is recycled, but most of it is not.

Although it is difficult to prove planned obsolescence as an industrial strategy, France made it illegal in 2015.

**B** 次の文が動画の内容に対して正しければ True に、誤っていれば False に ☑ をつけましょう。

1. Bernard London thought planned obsolescence should be an illegal strategy.   ☑ True   ☑ False

2. Software obsolescence is when a computer becomes unusable.   ☑ True   ☑ False

3. Screen manufacturing accounts for 80% of the environmental impact of smartphones.   ☑ True   ☑ False

**C** 次の文は動画の内容に関するものです。誤りが含まれているので、その箇所を抜き出して修正してみましょう。

1. Making repairs to a product easy is one form of planned obsolescence.

→

2. Most waste vanishes into the oceans, is stored in landfills, often in Africa, or incinerated.

→

## Communication Focus

### talking about similarities and differences　類似点・相違点を話す

　私たちは日常的にいろいろな比較をします。2つのものを比べる表現で重要なのは「～と同じくらい」と「より～」です。2つのものの程度が同じくらいなら、〈as 形容詞 as〉や〈the same 名詞 as〉を使います。一方が他方と比べて程度が高い（低い）ことをいう場合には〈比較級 than〉や〈not as 形容詞 as〉を使います。

- My old jacket looks just as good as <u>my brother's new one</u>.
  「私の古いジャケット、見た目はお兄さんの新しいのと同じくらいすてきでしょ。」

- My bicycle is about the same size as <u>this one</u>.「私の自転車はこれと同じくらいの大きさだよ。」

- The population of Tokyo is larger than <u>that of Osaka</u>.「東京の人口は大阪（の人口）より多い。」

- My watch is not as expensive as <u>the one you have</u>.「私の時計はあなたのほど高価ではない。」

　比較表現をするときに便利なのは、代名詞の one (ones) と that です。one は何らかの限定詞と共に（the one、this one、that one など）、that は前出のものを指して that of ... のように使います。上記の例の下線部に注目してみてください。

## Model Conversation

**A**　音声を聞きながら、次の会話を読んでみましょう。  2-29 Audio

Lee: I'm thinking of changing my phone.

Helen: Really, what's wrong with it?

Lee: Oh, not much. But I prefer the new improved version.

Helen: But isn't your old one smaller and easier to carry?

Lee: Well, it's ¹**about** the same size, but the screen on the new one is bigger.

Helen: But won't the new one ²**cost more** than the old one?

Lee: Yes, it will, but there is a ³**larger** choice of colors these days…

Helen: …Hey, isn't that just a ⁴**strategy** to make you keep buying new phones?

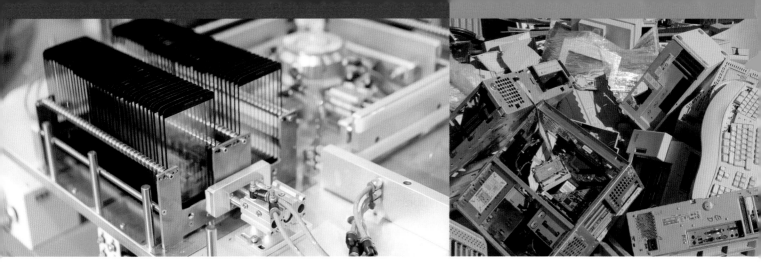

**B** Aの会話の太字部分の語句を下の語句と置きかえてペアで会話をしましょう。

| | | | |
|---|---|---|---|
| 1 | roughly | approximately | around |
| 2 | be more expensive | be priced higher | be more costly |
| 3 | greater | bigger | wider |
| 4 | tactic | scheme | way |

**C** ペアになって次の会話と同じ質問をしてみましょう。そして、例のように質問の回答を下の表に記入しましょう。

What do you like most about your phone?

What kind of phone will you get next time?

The camera: it takes amazing pictures!

I'd like one with a bigger screen.

| Partner's Name | What do you like most about your phone? | What kind of phone will you get next time? |
|---|---|---|
| 1 Bonnie | *the camera–amazing pictures* | *a phone with a bigger screen* |
| 2 | | |
| 3 | | |
| 4 | | |

# Thinking About the Topic

次の意見に対して、自分が賛成なら agree に、反対なら disagree に☑をつけましょう。

1. Planned obsolescence is bad for the economy.     ☑ agree   ☑ disagree

2. Planned obsolescence is good for the environment.     ☑ agree   ☑ disagree

3. I change my phone each time an improved version is available.     ☑ agree   ☑ disagree

4. Two years is a long time to use the same phone.     ☑ agree   ☑ disagree

5. Shipping electrical waste products to Africa is the right thing to do.     ☑ agree   ☑ disagree

# Talking About Your Idea

次の Discussion Starter の回答として自分の意見に近いほうを選び、その英文を完成させ、ペアかグループで発表しましょう。

| Discussion Starter | Buying a new phone helps the economy. |
| --- | --- |

**Partner 1's Opinion**

> I enjoy buying the latest model.

Reasons to support my idea

1. New phones are more energy efficient _____.

2. I can work faster with a new phone _____.

3. Manufacturers need to sell phones _____.

**Partner 2's Opinion**

> I am not sure what to do with my old phone.

Reasons to support my idea

1. I do not know where to recycle it _____.

2. My old phone contains a dangerous battery _____.

3. There are valuable metals in phones _____.

**クラス用DVD有り（別売）**

**クラス用音声CD有り（別売）**

# EarthWatch

### 動画で学んで発信するグローバル・イシュー

2020年1月20日　初版発行

2022年1月20日　第 3 刷

| | |
|---|---|
| 著　者 | Graeme Todd / Roger Palmer / 加野まきみ |
| 発行者 | 松村達生 |
| 発行所 | センゲージ ラーニング株式会社 |

〒102-0073　東京都千代田区九段北1-11-11　第2フナトビル5階

電話 03-3511-4392

FAX 03-3511-4391

e-mail: elt@cengagejapan.com

copyright © 2020 センゲージ ラーニング株式会社

| | |
|---|---|
| 装丁・組版 | 藤原志麻（クリエイド・ラーニング株式会社） |
| 編集協力 | クリエイド・ラーニング株式会社 |
| 本文イラスト | イチカワ エリ |
| 印刷・製本 | 株式会社ムレコミュニケーションズ |

ISBN 978-4-86312-370-0